Disability and Bridging the Digital Divide

ICT Accessibility and Assistive Technology

For People of All Abilities

By Nabil Eid

Table of Contents

FOREWORD

I have enjoyed working with Nabil Eid on programs to support individuals with disabilities worldwide. I met him on social media during our weekly AXSChat community.

His contributions to the chat have added value to many people. He lives in Syria, and despite all the problems in his country, he has dedicated his life to helping ensure that persons with disabilities are meaningfully included in education, employment, and society.

Most of his efforts have been focused on Arabic-speaking countries in the Middle East.

Society's role is to assure full access to education, secondary education, and employment. We also need to ensure that our houses, transportation, internet, communications, and technology (ICT) are accessible to everyone.

Society benefits when all members can participate to achieve their goals. Persons with Disabilities want to join the workforce and become taxpayers. Employers benefit by including persons with disabilities in their workforce. A more diverse workforce fosters innovation and cooperation.

Technological innovations also create unlimited possibilities for individuals with disabilities to contribute significantly and enable them to follow their life path. There are so many examples, but here are a few inventions that can change lives, including those of persons with disabilities.

Including individuals with disabilities has many moving parts, and the efforts must be blended into every aspect of society, from education, employment, transportation, housing, and socialization. Inclusion of people with disabilities is a civil rights issue, and we must also consider accessibility and Universal access.

Universal accessibility in the Information, Communication, and Technology (ICT) sector holds unparalleled promise and opportunity for persons with disabilities that have never been seen before.

Many people are surprised to learn just how much of the world's population is affected by a disability and how valuable the accessible design of ICT is to the global marketplace. According to the World Health Organization, 1 in 7 people have a disability, which equates to over 1 billion people.

It is also important to note that disabilities are a normal part of life. Persons with disabilities are not broken; they just might navigate the world differently. We all can add value when allowed to tap into our unique innate abilities. Accessible ICT is an important part of that equalizing equation.

To understand the impact, one has to look no further than the World Health Organization, which indicates that persons with disabilities are the world's largest and fastest-growing minority group. With the population of the United States aging and the likelihood of developing a disability or other mobility limitation increasing with age, the growth in the number of persons with disabilities continues to be expected to rise dramatically.

This is an exciting time with great promise and opportunity for people of all abilities. It is a new era for global citizens, where emerging technologies and mobile computing devices enable people of all ages and levels of education. Designing and delivering fully accessible ICT ensures that all individuals can enjoy the benefits and advantages of technology to enrich their lives and fulfill their dreams.

An inclusive, accessible, and universal design approach to technology is critical to both public and private industries that wish to anticipate the future needs of this growing population. By recognizing the importance of protecting and promoting the rights and dignity of persons with disabilities through assistive technology and accessible ICT, the world continues to strengthen policies, strategies, and programs, along with an increase in public awareness of the importance of the full inclusion of individuals with disabilities, accessible ICT, and assistive technology.

Experts report that the most obvious and cost-effective solutions are often ignored or overlooked, a mistake organizations and governmental bodies can no longer make when serving all citizens equally. Making technology usable for all has become imperative for unleashing the potential of all persons. It is critical for any public and private institution that hopes to fully participate and remain relevant in the 21st century.

Think about what you can do to reach persons with disabilities better, and find creative ways to make it happen through accessible technology. Move beyond general steps to protect and promote the rights of persons with disabilities, ensure that accessibility is addressed in all policies and programs, promote training on the human rights of persons with disabilities, stop any practice that breaches the rights of persons with disabilities, and involve persons with disabilities in the development of legislation and policies.

Nabil has written on the many topics impacting persons with disabilities. His writing maps out the steps needed to fully include people with disabilities in all aspects of society and implement the United Nations Convention on the Rights of Persons with Disabilities (CRPD).

Nabil Eid is one of the greatest minds in our industry. I hope his writing inspires you as much as it has inspired me.

Debra Ruh
Global Disability Inclusion Strategist,
CEO of Ruh Global IMPACT,
Co-Founder AXSChat,
Debra@RuhGlobal.com, www.RuhGlobal.com

INTRODUCTION

 Information and Communication Technology (ICT) is an enabling technology, and we should not lose sight of this fact. It might put us into social gaps or the `Digital Divide' if it is not properly planned, managed, and implemented. I strongly believe that all of us are here because we all agree that none of us should be left out in isolation in this highly useful and challenging digital world. ICT accessibility is very important to all of us, especially to persons with disabilities.

15% of the world's population lives with a disability. This represents about 1 billion people globally. (ICTs) and assistive technologies are a unique infrastructure that expands access to key public services, promoting digital inclusion. Persons with disabilities already benefit from the advantages of ICT-enabled applications and AT services; to the benefit of ICTs for all, ICTs have to be made accessible to persons with disabilities, so these technologies constitute an opportunity and not a barrier.

This book gives an overview of disability and bridging the digital divide for people of all abilities. The focus is on using e-accessibility, Assistive Technology, and accessible ICTs to support persons with disabilities. The development of modern Assistive Technology (AT) offers unprecedented access to information and communication and improves the functional capabilities of persons with disabilities.

An accessible ICT product or service can be used by all of its intended users, taking into account their differing capabilities. Accessible ICTs have the potential to provide persons with disabilities unprecedented levels of access to education, skills training, and employment, as well as the opportunity to participate in the economic, cultural, and social life of their community. Accessible ICTs from the access to ICTs gap perspective is often seen as universal access and may be regarded as the first important step in addressing accessible ICTs.

Therefore, due to the importance of such studies, I am very happy to share my book and offer it for free. The E-Book contains extensive articles and studies of how persons with disabilities have used ICT accessibility and assistive technology in access and Inclusion through technology.

Finally, I am convinced we can make ICT accessibility a reality worldwide. Together, we can set the stage for effective multi-stakeholder engagement in promoting accessible ICTs, an essential enabler of the rights of persons with disabilities in information society and our digital world.

Nabil Eid

Teleworking for employment of persons with disabilities

Working at home, sometimes called remote working, teleworking, or telecommuting, is an important option for many persons with disabilities because it allows for more flexibility and may only be possible to produce better results than working in a conventional workplace. It seeks jobs and work hours from home to make money online. It is a potential form of employment for persons with disabilities, provided care is taken over by the selection of workers, identification of work suited to the telework format, and management of telework units by employers.

Teleworking can be much simpler for dealing with all persons with disabilities (visible or invisible), whatever accessible workplace, and attitudes at an office or other place of work. A new survey around telecommuting indicates that 81% of professionals with disabilities would like to telework, at least part-time.

Today's ICT innovation is changing the world. The world of Assistive Technology (AT) and high-speed Internet access means new choices and good-paying options for people who want the flexibility and convenience of careers that don't require commuting to an office or working for someone else. New technologies and innovations in ICT accessibility help create solutions for accessible workplaces that increase productivity, flexibility, and creative thinking.

Technological advancements have helped increase telework options, which can also result in expanded options and opportunities for persons with disabilities.

Recent studies have indicated that home-based telework is a very flexible form of employment. It may involve working from a home base for part of each week and from a conventional office for the rest of the week, working from home on specific elements of a broader workload that are suited to the telework format, or working at home for most of the time, with occasional visits to the company offices. The feasibility of home-based telework for persons with disabilities in a variety of forms has been demonstrated in many studies, taking into consideration several conditions needed to be realized in the management of telework arrangements by the employing organization, responsibility for maintaining contact with the teleworker and for monitoring the performance of work.

Accordingly, persons with disabilities as teleworkers should be qualified to do the work; they need a training approach, and induction training may be necessary where they are new employees of the employing organization. The period of induction serves two purposes: besides familiarizing the teleworker with the type of service provided by the organization, it also enables them to get to know other employees of the organization and make links which are essential to prevent feelings of isolation from developing, when the teleworking arrangements become operative.

What are the benefits of teleworking for persons with disabilities?

Employment of persons with disabilities to work from home is a growing trend. Companies and workers recognize the benefits of providing opportunities for certain employees to skip commuting to the office and work from home.

The following are some of the benefits of teleworking:

- For complex needs and some persons with disabilities, working at home may be their only employment possibility.
- It brings many employment opportunities for persons with disabilities and saves significant time that would otherwise be used commuting, especially for those who need accessible transportation services.
- Reasonable accommodation at the lowest cost for employers and employees with disabilities allows employers to attract and retain valuable workers by boosting employee morale and productivity.
- Ability to work outside of standard hours: working hours are often flexible, and employer teleworking policies vary; some require a virtual presence between specific hours, while others have no concern about when work is completed.
- Arrangements can be quite flexible, ranging from examples in which work is performed mainly from home to those that combine home-based activity with varying degrees of conventional office-based activity.
- It is easier to manage their disabilities at home and flexible to change positions due to better access to attendant services. They can also produce better results than working in a conventional workplace.

- Teleworking is a possible form of employment for persons with disabilities, provided care is taken over the selection of workers, identification of work suited to the telework format, and management of telework units by employers.

ICT accessibility and Teleworking

Gaining access to ICT ensures that persons with disabilities will succeed in their teleworking positions. The most important factor for them in teleworking positions is the understanding that to participate in the workforce fully, persons with disabilities must have access to and use information and data comparable to the access and use by applicants and employees without disabilities.

This is especially true about recruiting individuals with disabilities for teleworking positions. If persons with disabilities are not provided with accessible ICT, they are limited in their ability to develop skills needed to be productive team members and advance in employment. A commitment to accessible and usable ICT is essential to facilitating meaningful and effective teleworking opportunities.

Successful teleworking strategies, especially for employees with disabilities, cannot be implemented adequately without proper training and job support. Training should be implemented for both employers and employees with disabilities. To work effectively in teleworking positions, employees need to use effective customer service skills, problem-solving techniques, computer skills, and communication skills. Next, training on using these skills will allow employees with disabilities to assess better the skills needed for teleworking and evaluate their need for assistive technology and ICT accessibility in completing job tasks in a telework position.

In this context, persons with disabilities should have the same opportunity to telework as persons without disabilities. Teleworking policies are inclusive when they do not include barriers to employees and candidates with disabilities. Working from home is ideal for many of them, making it easier to work around the effects of a disability and create new opportunities for people with severe disabilities, as well as enabling others who become disabled during employment to retain their jobs. Many companies have an almost untapped talent pool waiting for jobs.

However, these individuals are largely ignored because they can't or are less able to commute to the office.

A good teleworking policy lays the groundwork for successful telework arrangements for persons with and without disabilities.

If your organization doesn't have an established teleworking policy, it's time to develop one. If your organization already has a teleworking policy, you can devote more time to the planning required to implement individual telework requests successfully.

Accessible banking to persons with disabilities

"Technology is important in the lives of persons with disabilities; we should not lose sight of the fact that more Accessible means more Inclusion, provide persons with disabilities with appropriate technology, support their well-being, and continue to build and embed an inclusive culture and enable them to realize their potential."

According to WHO and the World Bank, about 15.3 percent of the world's population, or one billion persons, live with some form of disability. Persons with disabilities tend to be acutely vulnerable to exclusion.

Yes! 1.3 billion is a significant percentage of the world's population.

Unfortunately, many are not given equal financial inclusion opportunities in financial products and services as their peers. They are denied their rights to be integral to the financial inclusion community.

Full financial inclusion means access to a suite of financial services; persons with disabilities would like to be treated as "normal," able, and capable of accessing financial services.

Financial Institutions working with people with disabilities should accept and respect this fact and make their decision to provide financial assistance accordingly.

We admit that financial services regulation is complex, and making sense of financial inclusion policy and regulation requires a great deal of creativity, especially given all the different factors that supervisors must consider beyond prudential supervision, but that is not impossible! All Member States are responsible for achieving social justice through the protection of the equal rights of their citizens, including persons with disabilities, education, science, culture, communication, and financial inclusion using various technological solutions.

The Convention on the Rights of Persons with Disabilities-CRPD

The Convention on the Rights of Persons with Disabilities (CRPD) has paved the way for promoting accessibility in all public services, including financial services. CRPD contains several provisions that refer to people with disabilities and accessibility to banking services.

- Article 9 deals with accessibility, and clause 2. b affirms that the state should ensure that private entities that offer open facilities and services to the public consider all aspects of accessibility for persons with disabilities.
- Article 12 affirms the right of persons with disabilities to have equal recognition before the law. Clause 5 addresses the right of persons with disabilities to control their financial affairs and have equal access to financial credit and loans.
- With the Government trying to make persons with disabilities more independent by promoting better education and employment, it is important that they can manage their financial affairs and take an important step towards living an independent life.

Limited Access to Financial Services

In several countries, specifically developing countries, persons with different types of disabilities cannot independently open and operate bank accounts, access loans, or use electronic and online banking facilities. They have limited access to financial services, including traditional and alternative banking, online payment services and financial transactions, and mobile banking; many have faced challenges in accessing and using financial services, from policy barriers to the inaccessibility of financial institutions.

This is primarily based on assumptions about what persons with disabilities can and cannot do, their capacity to read and write, and their ability to make important financial decisions independently; also, many policies within financial institutions do not promote access to all persons. Policies around authentication and lack of enforcement and governance continue to challenge many organizations, including financial organizations, in their ability and resilience to be accessible and inclusive.

In today's world, access to financial services for all is necessary, not simply at the community or household level but at an individual level, to open doors to banking services, credit services, stocks and shares, insurance, and other markets. Access to and inclusion in financial services is crucial to poverty reduction and participation in economic prosperity, growth, and development.

ICT accessibility to enable financial services

Technological advances and ICT accessibility have changed how financial services are publicized, offered, and used, among other issues. The growing availability and use of Internet banking, phone, and mobile banking generate greater expectations of receiving services "anywhere, anytime" and drive perceptions that everyone can now access banking services through various devices and digital solutions.

Persons with disabilities now demand better and easier access to the entire range of financial services through ICT accessibility, ensuring and increasing an inclusive workplace for employees, maximizing technology advances, and diversity inclusion for all.

There are a large number of persons in the world with different levels of disability who will benefit from technology-based banking services, with many receiving independent access for the first time.

The increasing nature of services now available through technology has triggered growing demand among persons who remained marginalized from traditional paper-based banking services; there is increased evidence that integrating accessibility in the design of products and services from the start results in cost savings and more streamlined and efficient processes that enhance customer experience. By offering an online experience through any device personalized to individual needs, preferences, and abilities, organizations can reach the broadest population base, especially the "unbanked" and "under-banked," to enhance interactions and improve sales opportunities.

For example, some technology-enabled financial services, such as SMS-based mobile money services for rural areas, e-banking, mobile banking, and phone-based banking, offer significant opportunities for persons with disabilities and diverse abilities to access various services through multiple mediums. On the other hand, if technology-enabled services are poorly designed, they will create a larger digital divide and further exclude persons with diverse abilities from critical and necessary access to financial services.

eAccessibility to banking services

'eAccessibility' concerns the design and supply of Information and Communication.

Technology (ICT) products and services should be designed to be accessible to people with disabilities and others for whom the technical features of ICTs pose barriers to usage.

The full spectrum of ICTs needs to be accessible if everyone is to have equal opportunities for participation in everyday social and economic life in the Information Society. This includes ICT products such as computers, telephones, and the wide range of other ICT devices now part of everyday life, ICT-based network services such as telephony and TV, the many web-based and phone-based services that are in everyday use today such as online government and shopping, call centers and so on and other ICT-based modes of service delivery such as financial services by mobile banking, Internet banking and self-service terminals like ATMs and ticket machines. Focus on persons with different types of disabilities to promote accessibility for E-Banking services such as:

Telephone banking solutions

Telephone banking could be very useful if the proper tools are available to persons with disabilities. For instance, hearing, speech, and even dexterity impairments may face several barriers to successfully using telephone banking services. In some cases, getting in touch with someone on the other end can be difficult, if not completely unavailable.

- **Providing text transmitter equipment:** Calls using text transmitter equipment. Deaf or hard of hearing customers, or those with speech disabilities, may contact the customer Line with questions about access to the bank and requests about products and services.

- **Telephone transfer service:** For customers who cannot visit a branch or who are not presently using online banking services, the bank may offer a telephone transfer service through which certain transactions can be made, including funds transfers among bank accounts, balance inquiries, certain stop payments, etc. (*Apple Bank for saving*).

- **Interactive Voice Response (IVR):** Employ (IVR) technology or touch-tone features of the user's phone and ensure that IVR systems can work well with TTY or provide standalone TTY numbers for telephone banking. For example, suppose a person with a hearing or speech impairment cannot use the IVR system. In that case, they should be given alternative input options, including touch-tone dialing or requesting an operator.

- **Video relay services:** Video relay services facilitate consumer telephone banking using sign language.
- **Manual operators:** Provide manual operators and signal their availability to callers early in the call.
- **Mobile banking services:** Telephone banking can be combined with mobile banking services such as SMS to facilitate customer ease of access.

Internet banking solutions

Internet banking could provide the best solutions. Accessible Internet banking has the potential to make a very big difference to many persons with disabilities in addition to the advantages it provides for the population as a whole.

Internet banking can provide people with accessibility problems with other means of banking (such as access to a "walk-in" branch or telephone banking), a means to remain independent and more in control of their financial requirements.

The Internet banking standard includes:

- Transactions include online service registration, balance inquiry, statement viewing, transfer between accounts, bill pay, third-party funds transfer, reviewing and updating investments and portfolios, online loan applications, and interactive financial calculations.
- Email associated with the delivery of Internet banking services.
- Dependencies that can impact the effective accessibility and usability of online services for the financial institution, web development tools, user's minimum hardware and software expectations, and reliance on scripting and applet technologies. In addition, for the customer, level of experience, platforms and operating systems, assistive technology brand and version, firewalls, connections, etc.

The biggest obstacle to developing Internet banking options that are accessible to all is the wide diversity of people who are trying to access the banks' websites with or without assistive technologies or aids. Universal design comes into play here. Also, one of the main barriers to web accessibility is that designers and web developers are often unaware of accessibility practices.

Many websites may not work with assistive technologies, thus preventing disabled users from accessing services or functions.

The goal of universal design is to have each web page accessible by all persons; the website for banking should be Accessibility standards WCAG2.0. This is of concern when we talk about banks and financial institutions run by various governments that need to comply with these standards and guidelines, as they cater to a large population of customers with disabilities.

Internet banking could provide the best solution; banks can make websites more accessible and follow the prescribed guidelines, such as WCAG2.0 and usability principles, to ensure a better banking experience with adequate security not just for their customers with disabilities but all customers.

Internet banking offerings can be made accessible through the following:

- Ensuring accessibility guidelines in developing mobile applications, website interfaces, and mobile content such (WCAG2.0)

- Ensuring access without a mouse through assistive technology such as screen readers and voice recognition software.

- Ensure documentation, including statements in print or pen and digital formats like HTML or RTF. It also offers accessible and alternative formats such as audio, large-size fonts, accessible e-text or DAISY formats, and Braille printables.

- Thoroughly test the websites before deployment and provide accessible means for consumers to provide feedback on any accessibility barriers.

- Offer alternatives to CAPTCHA, such as audio codes or math questions, to ensure independent login processes.

- Offer real-time access to customer service representatives through instant chat, video conferencing with captions, or video relay services that enable real-time sign language interpretation. Provide a hotline service to assist customers with navigating and using Internet banking facilities.

Automatic Teller Machines (ATMs) Solutions

(ATM) - a wall-mounted, stand-alone, or semi-secure electronic terminal that is customer-activated and designed to perform basic transactions such as cash withdrawal and balance inquiry and advanced transactions such as cheque deposits, bill payments, and transfers between accounts.

Deployment and operation of ATM solutions by using standards to cover issues of physical and technology accessibility for ATMs, define accessibility requirements for ATMs and ATM sites, and make the product or environment more usable; some persons with disabilities may have requirements that cannot be met within the standard.

Focus on how accessibility can be mainstreamed into ATM design.

- **Accessible physical access:** ATMs' height and reach should be appropriate for different users, including those who use wheelchairs.

- **Visibility and lighting:** ATMs should be physically accessible, have proper lighting, and have signage in appropriate formats, including Braille, large print, and tactile signs.

- **Talking ATMs:** These feature speech output capabilities to provide accessibility to blind and visually impaired customers and voice instructions accessible through headphones inserted into an ATM jack.

- **Universal keyboard layout and Braille decals:** To assist blind or visually impaired persons, ATM keyboards should have a universal design, with a dimple for the "5" key and special raised symbols for locating the ATM's cancel, enter, and clear keys. In addition, Braille decals identify the major components on the ATM face, including the receipt printer, deposit, and dispenser slots.

Banking accessibility and ATMs are examples of barriers

Here are the results of the Disabled People's Association (DPA) survey about Access to Banking Services in 2013. The study aimed to assess barriers and difficulties persons with disabilities may experience while accessing banking services.

- Many banks do not allow blind customers to operate individual accounts and insist they operate joint accounts with family members instead.

- Banks rely on signatures for some transactions. For people who are blind, signatures are often not a good means of verification, as blind people tend to have less consistent signatures.

- While the general banking services, apart from phone banking, are generally accessible to people who are hard of hearing, the main barrier experienced by people is the lack of non-auditory means for emergency/helpline communications.

- Choose a bank based on accessibility features rather than on favorable terms or conditions or banking solutions that suit their needs.

- A generation of people with hearing impairment are illiterate and unable to use internet banking.

- ATMs are inaccessible to the blind as information feedback is largely visible through the ATM display. Touchscreen/dynamic displays, while providing more functions to the sighted users, are completely inaccessible to the blind.

- Displays on ATMs are too small to cater to people with impaired vision, and strong sunlight can cause glares on the ATM display, making the ATM inaccessible to users with impaired vision.

- Software upgrades for online and mobile banking often render the system inaccessible.

- Replacement of ATM cards needs telephone intervention

Also, the report "Inclusive financial services for seniors and persons with disabilities: Global Trends in Accessibility Requirements" is available in G3ict for more information about understanding the barriers to inaccessible financial services for people with different disabilities.

Accessibility training and awareness staff about banking and financial services

Accessibility training for all customer-facing employees to educate them about Accessibility services and properly serving all customers, including those with disabilities, will be provided to staff and contract workers whose duties involve interaction with the public or third parties.
Training will include:
- Accessibility standards related to ATMs, net banking, assistive technology aids, and several other aspects of banking accessibility.

- The fundamental principle of an Accessible ATM for development and Industry Standards for ATMs.

- Standards document on Accessible ATMs for customers with disabilities.

- Standards for financial inclusion.

- Policies and standards that promote better access to financial services.
- WCAG2.0 standards for website accessibility.
- How to interact and communicate with persons with various types of disability who use an assistive device or require assistance

Training must also be provided continuously regarding changes to banking policies, practices, and procedures.

Accessibility and the future of the Internet of Things

Smartphones, cloud computing, and the Internet of Things (IoT) are being harnessed in increasingly innovative ways to enhance people's quality of life, expand their access to the Internet, and enhance their participation in the Internet governance ecosystem.

Internet-connected devices, known as the Internet of Things (IoT), offer similar potential to transform the quality of life for many people, particularly those with disabilities and older people. (IoT) is a phrase for everyday objects connected to the internet and participating in a system. However, it also means converging conventional connected devices and smart appliances. This has very useful applications for persons with disabilities where all applications such as smart mobile Apps, smart home applications, smart transportation, remote health care, and smart environment, in addition to more objects at home such as smart mirrors, Smart window air conditioner, chairs, books, keys, cups, egg minder, smart sensors mother, etc., may be connected to the Internet and interact with other objects and with people exchanging information through the Internet. This has very useful devices and applications for persons with disabilities, connecting objects and people to objects.

The various applications that manage the devices in the IOT decide which command and control is best for the conditions and provide the necessary information.

However, the Internet of Things is happening now. It promises to offer a revolutionary, fully connected "smart" world as the relationships between objects, their environment, and people become more tightly intertwined. Yet the issues and challenges associated with IoT must be addressed to realize the potential benefits for individuals, society, and the economy.

An Overview Understanding the Issues and challenges of a more connected world.

The emergence of the Internet of Things is an exciting development for everyone. We are particularly excited to see how innovators can use this new technological revolution to empower persons with disabilities and open new opportunities, giving them unprecedented control of their environment.

Accessibility requirements for IoT

From the accessibility point of view, the ideal setting would be a unique global infrastructure for the Internet of Things, controlled by the mentioned central body, with several service providers that could be accessed from different platforms. These platforms would be responsible for implementing accessibility needed to ensure universal access.

Accessibility requirements for IoT devices present new challenges, as new devices must be introduced while remaining compatible with existing accessibility standards and guidelines. We don't yet know the precise form and function of how IoT can break accessibility barriers. What is known is that inclusive design needs to be a fundamental element in creating IoT-enabled smart environments.

Adopting a philosophy of creating an enabling environment through IoT, which embodies inclusiveness rather than just a smart environment, will ensure inclusion in our technological future.

Most of the enabling technologies for the IoT already exist (some do not have optimal form or function yet but can contribute to the IoT). Based on this, the key driver for the adoption of IoT lies in the applications and new ways of solving existing challenges.

Not all aspects of IoT have been resolved to the point of seamless integration. Some challenges remain. The most significant of these are privacy, trust, and security aspects. Some applications of the Internet of People, such as the Social Web, have partially answered some of these aspects. Still, introducing objects to the Internet adds complexity to resource sharing, attribution, and usage management. In the IoT world, the question of who can see and act on what remains unanswered.

An important aspect to be considered is the interface through which the information is obtained on objects of the Internet of Things. Data must be available through various communication channels and adapted to the functional diversity of the person using and accessing it. For example, in the case of a deaf person, data can be made available through written text, but it should not reach that person through audio with synthesized text. On the contrary, in the case of a blind person, ideally, the channel should be just the opposite; getting data through an audio channel is preferable to a written text. See how you envisage the "governance" of such an organization. "Internet of Things" (IoT).

Interoperability and accessibility are key principles that must be part of the IoT governance principles. Governance authorities responsible for these services must be involved in IoT governance mechanisms. A multi-stakeholder platform may also be able to address IoT governance issues.

Implementing the IoT governance framework requires 'hard approaches' to enforce accessibility features and 'soft approaches' that can be responsive to industry requirements in a fast-moving environment.

An integrated solution addressing four technological gaps, see Inclusion Through the Internet of Things.

- How can the environment be made aware of its state?
- How to model the context in a virtual system?
- How do we provide intelligent services based on learning and reasoning?
- How do we computationally manage this connected and integrated environment?

The IoT could have an immeasurable impact on people with disabilities and help dramatically improve their quality of life. As connected devices become even more pervasive, the potential for people with disabilities becomes even greater, and app developers will have to spend considerable time on the user interface (UI).

The Internet of Things' potential can help enable assistive technologies and increase accessibility support and services for persons with disabilities in domains such as service provision, health care, job integration, education and learning, independent and assisted living, and navigation and mobility support in public spaces, including public transport, cultural places, and shopping for goods.

The future promises greater inclusion by integrating IoT services and technologies upfront.

By raising awareness of societal needs now, we can live in a more inclusive world tomorrow.

Telecare, Assistive technology, and ICT accessibility for persons with Dementia

"Don't forget the elderly people; they need lots of hands, love, and support."

The proportion of older people in our society is growing at an unprecedented rate, and with life expectancy also increasing, more and more people are likely to be affected.

The number of persons with dementia will double in the next 40 years, and the number of those 85+ with dementia will triple.

One key response to this emerging challenge has been the development of assistive technologies designed to help people with dementia live independently and safely for longer and reduce the pressure on their carers.

It's important to note that assistive technology is not about the technology. Instead, it is about enhancing a person's quality of life through improved outcomes in safeguarding, living standards, social interaction, and greater independence.

Assistive technology aims to support people with dementia and their carers at home. Introducing technology into residential facilities can have major benefits. Both people with dementia and staff benefit as jobs are made safer, easier, and more supportive of person-centered care. Assistive technology ranges from simple things like walking sticks to sophisticated equipment like satellite-based navigation systems to find people who have walked away from facilities. It includes kitchen technologies for residential care, nursing aids, and new administrative software. Technology is useful at many levels.

Using Assistive Technology

Assistive technology can help and enable people with dementia to live more independently. It may not be the answer for everybody, but some products can be useful for many people. Using assistive technology depends on a person's needs and environmental factors. Personal factors include the level and stage of cognitive impairment, ability to carry out activities of daily living, emotional factors like anxiety or depression, and wanting to walk away from a facility.

Environmental factors include the capacity of building structures, the design of new facilities, the relevance of technologies, staff training, family members' understanding of the benefits of technology, and management commitment to long-term benefits despite high initial costs.

Benefits of assistive technology

A range of products is available, and assistive technologies help persons with dementia communicate, remind, and maintain safety in their homes.

Assistive technologies that are successful in domestic settings are useful in facilities.

For example:

- Improve quality of life.
- Increased choice, safety, and independence allow persons with dementia to make more decisions.
- Offer safer and more secure living.
- Give people more privacy and dignity.
- Reassure family members about the level and quality of care and reduce the burden on carers.
- Offset the need for some personal care.
- Improve support for people with long-term health conditions.

Assistive Technology Tools for Persons with Dementia

Assistive technologies include more tools such as computers, smart wiring, alarms, automated door openers, smart stove-tops, and Smart toilets.

Other technologies include hidden switches and control lockouts, electric strikes, and reed switches outside doors, which allow people to move freely without staff supervision.

Sensors are another safety-related technology; they can detect extreme temperatures, scalding baths, gas, falls, absences from bed or chair, and nighttime disturbances.

Assistive technology for everyday living includes automatic lighting control, stove-top monitors and shut-offs, automatic taps that turn off if users forget, time-orientation support, and place and time reminders.

ICT accessibility and Dementia

ICT accessibility and advances in computer technology make it easier for persons with impairments to use better access. These include:

- Larger keys or keyboards, different key displays, and onscreen keyboards.
- Touch screens rather than a mouse or keyboard.
- Screen enlargers and screen magnifiers.
- Speech and voice recognition programs rather than a mouse or keyboard.
- Screen readers read everything on the screen, including text, graphics, control buttons, and menus.
- Software programs that use speech synthesizers for auditory feedback about what is being typed.

ICT and multimedia can promote more meaningful contact between staff and people with dementia. For example, people can look at databases of video clips, music, songs, and photographs together. Using a touch screen, users have limited choices and can pick the media format they want.

Multimedia technology can help with cognitive issues. For example, it can create reminiscences, support enjoyable experiences, and give options for success and mastery.

Additional ICT accessibility tools include wireless nurse-call systems, wireless laptops, palm pilots to collect and send data, emergency call systems, and computers wired from unit to unit in cluster-designed facilities.

Technological innovations for persons with Dementia

List of the top tech innovations on the market today for persons with dementia and their caregivers:

Reminder Messages

Reminders can help keep properties and loved ones safe when the caregiver can't. These messages are recorded on a device in the home and then played back out loud at the appropriate time. For example, a caregiver may record a message to play that reminds a person to take a medication at the correct time. Some devices can play messages depending on the person's activity. For example, if someone with dementia leaves their home, a reminder message could tell them to lock the front door. This technology can also remind both caregiver and patient of appointments. Other reminder messages can also let those who have dementia know not to open the door, to go back to bed, and to provide reassurance when the caregiver is not present.

Clocks

Clocks specifically designed for those with Alzheimer's and dementia can help ease the anxiety associated with a diagnosis. Someone with dementia may confuse night and day, and an easy-to-read clock can help them distinguish the time. This can also help caregivers try to set a routine by showing their loved one that it is the time they say it is.

Medication Management

Medication management technology can be as simple as a pillbox marked with days of the week or as high-tech as automated pill dispensers that beep and open to remind caregivers and those with dementia to take their medication. Some medication reminders are as simple as a vibrating alarm on a watch. This technology serves busy caregivers well by allowing them to trust the device for a medication reminder.

GPS Location and Tracking Devices

Location tracking devices are a great option for those with dementia who may wander. Tracking devices can be worn or attached to the person in some way, and many have alert systems that let caregivers know if their loved one has left a certain area. This technology can also alert emergency personnel to ensure a speedy and safe recovery.

Picture Phones

They are specifically designed for people who cannot remember phone numbers and may need to contact someone quickly. These phones have large numbers and are pre-programmable with frequently called phone numbers. Some phones come with clear buttons where photos can be placed so that the person can just push the button associated with the photos to call their loved one quickly.

Electrical Use Monitoring

This new technology is designed for caregivers who do not live with their loved ones. It monitors their use of electrical appliances by plugging into a wall outlet or power strip. It will alert caregivers if their commonly used appliances have not been turned on or off.

Telecare for Persons with Dementia

Telecare is the remote or enhanced delivery of health and social services to people in their homes through telecommunications and computerized systems.

Telecare refers to equipment and detectors that provide continuous, automatic, and remote monitoring of care needs, emergencies, and lifestyle changes. These devices use information and communication technology (ICT) to trigger human responses or shut down equipment to prevent hazards.

ICT accessibility and Telecare for Persons with Dementia

The role of telecare in supporting someone living with dementia varies greatly. Telecare provides assistive technology that ranges from simple, standalone devices to complex, integrated systems that help a person remain independent for as long as possible. Some areas where telecare may help include everyday living, monitoring, safety, communication, and prompts and reminders.

Safety: Assistive technology for persons with dementia is primarily designed to support security and safety while providing a less intrusive living environment. For example, motion sensor technology can silently alert staff when residents with a high risk of falling move away from their chairs or beds to reduce the likelihood of falls and injuries.

Everyday living: Telecare can also assist with a person's daily needs.

AT gadgets may include temperature sensors for automatic climate control, lamp and light activation, automated ovens, dishwashers and washing machines, automatic window and curtain controls, floor cleaning robots, garden sensors for automated watering, and electronic showers, taps, and toilets. Point-of-care technologies also enable remote monitoring of a person's daily health condition, such as blood sugar, blood pressure, and heart rate.

This data can be automatically transmitted to the appropriate health professional, who can monitor vital signs and make appropriate decisions about necessary interventions.

Monitoring: In instances where a person with dementia is prone to wandering and disorientation, telecare provides assistive technology such as virtual door and exit sensors that detect entry and exit and can be implemented to alert family members, loved ones, and carers. GPS tracking devices can securely monitor the person's exact location within meters.

Communication enables carers to be on-hand and assist when necessary instead of providing round-the-clock, one-on-one supervision. For example, video conferencing is now being used to facilitate communication with health professionals and service providers, which is particularly important where an older person may reside at a significant distance from the health clinic. In this context, assistive technology has the potential to relieve the pressure on carers and support their efforts in delivering care in a way that promotes the independence of the resident or service user.

Online communication can also help address social isolation. For example, it enables older people to communicate with friends and relatives or participate in major family events via networked computers with internet capabilities. Access to internet applications and online browsing, research, learning, and games can also help broaden a person's interests.

Prompts and reminders: Incorporate personal solutions that positively impact confidence, health, and well-being. Examples include automatic medication dispensers that help people with dementia maintain medication compliance. In contrast, orientation clocks can help with confusion about the time, day of the week, month, or year, and locator devices help to find lost property items.

Accessible e-learning platforms, hopes, and challenges!

Technology has great potential to overcome physical barriers and improve access to learning for students with disabilities. The increased use of ICTs in most sectors of society and recent developments in adaptive hardware and software have allowed individuals with disabilities to do things that were difficult or impossible for them to do in the past.

Some empirical research exists on online learning for students with disabilities. Still, it is insufficient, leaving educators with many questions but no consensus about how best to serve such students in accessible content and an online environment.

The key element of e-learning and accessible content is how to ensure that online learning is accessible to the broadest spectrum of learners with disabilities and whether the lack of the proper environment represents a denial of a student's legal right to a free and appropriate education. UNESCO Global Report, 2013 indicates that persons with disabilities face a wide range of barriers, including access to information, education, and a lack of job opportunities. However, Information and Communication Technologies (ICT) can be a powerful tool in supporting education and inclusion for persons with disabilities.

Accessible eLearning, such as web-based courses, can be taken and completed successfully by learners with disabilities. Accessible e-learning creates an online learning experience that includes as many people as possible, regardless of their physical, sensory, or cognitive limitations. Still, the challenge of developing accessible content is developing e-learning for a corporation, academic institution, or government agency, so we must follow best practices when developing e-learning accessible to learners with disabilities. Following accessibility best practices will also help to create more usable courses for all learners. There are requirements for making electronic resources and information technology accessible to students with disabilities. These standards are based on guidelines originally developed by the Web Accessibility Initiative and known as WCAG2.0 and Authoring Tool Accessibility Guidelines (ATAG) 2.0.

In this context, we will examine how disability is activated differently online, the impact of this on learning and teaching through the internet, and the accessibility of two of the most popular learning management systems.

Accessibility problems are not just about online teaching platforms. As Guglielman (2010, 1) observed, e-learning needs to address accessibility and inclusion from both the perspective of technology and pedagogy. This is particularly true for students with disabilities. Accessible content is effectively used by people in the following disability groups: Blind or visually impaired, deaf, mobility impairments, and learning with disabilities students.

Good accessible design makes e-learning more accessible for everyone. Conversely, poor design can make content hard for all students with disabilities to access. There are several areas in which e-learning can work to the advantage of students with disabilities when studying in the context of education. These include accessibility, flexibility, and disclosure (Kent 2015, para 11). Online information can be available in various formats to best suit the person accessing it, whether visual through a screen displaying images or text, audio as spoken words and sound, or touch devices. For specific information on accessibility features and more about usable and accessible platforms, see examples such as Blackboard, Microsoft Lync, and Second Life.

According to the Americans with Disabilities Act, online courses should be accessible to students with disabilities. However, since the ADA does not provide specific accommodation standards, each school must decide how much it will serve its students with disabilities. In a perfect world, online courses should be created using universal design, the idea that all course material should be accessible in different ways, be it through audio, video, or text, says Vickie S. Cook, director of the Center for Online Learning, Research and Service at the University of Illinois—Springfield.

E-learning holds many possibilities for inclusion for persons with disabilities. However, the online platforms must provide access for all students.

Given this, making e-learning accessible should be a priority for schools and universities—the rising rates of online learning in education.

There are many accessibility options in e-learning, and we need to design courses that meet popular accessibility standards, such as Section 508 and the Web Content Accessibility Guidelines.

There are a set of questions that should be in consideration:

What are Section 508 and WCAG? How are they different?

What tools can you use to make your e-learning courses follow accessibility best practices and adhere to the law?

Have you ever thought about how someone with a disability experiences the online courses you create?

What if your target audience includes people who are deaf or hard of hearing, color blind, visually impaired (partially or totally), or have limited mobility? Shouldn't they be afforded the same learning opportunities and access to your courses?

For example, courses should be designed to navigate with keyboards, include alt text, images, and text on the screen for clarity, create highly usable course navigation, consider when including audio and video in courses, and ensure screencasts are accessible.

Accessibility of e-learning and free courses introduces challenges for students with disabilities who may use computers differently when taking part in e-learning or need alternative teaching methods. It covers the technology and techniques used by students with disabilities, the adjustments to teaching methods that might be reasonable, design decisions that affect the accessibility of e-learning tools, and strategies for evaluation. Many online courses are not designed with accessibility (Roberts, Crittenden & Crittenden 2011). This means that students who do not disclose that they have a disability may be disadvantaged. It also means that when students request accommodation to access the learning environment, a process of design-redesign is required to accommodate the students, adding additional costs. Hence, we need to understand the main challenges facing students with disabilities in eLearning and understanding of the types of technology used by students with disabilities.

Courses should be designed to be accessible from the beginning, and implementing universal design principles at the outset avoided costs caused by the need to engage in a digital retrofit. Also, the design learning platform includes multiple learning modalities that could be superior to in-person education for students with disabilities.

Here are six basic principles to consider when making an e-learning course accessible:

- Ensure that courses should be accessed using a screen reader and keyboard;
- Use HTML heading tags correctly;
- Provide transcripts or captions for video and audio content;
- Ensure that content has good color contrast;
- Create ALT tags to describe each image or diagram;
- Use inclusive language.

In addition, it is important to understand the basic principles of accessibility.

- All contents should be understandable in more than one perception stream.
- Users should maintain control of video speeds and simulations.

- Information in imagery should not purely be conveyed in color.

- Simulations and videos should also avoid "strobe effects," which may trigger seizures in some people.

- Information structures should be made clear to those using text readers

- Sites must be understandable even if users have shut down all imagery.

- Live online events and conferences would benefit from live captioning (if available).

- Tables should be created in a way that is easy to understand.

Most e-learning systems for learners with disabilities cannot deliver accessible learning content. However, learners with disabilities need everything to be accessible.

Online education can seem like a promising alternative for students with disabilities. However, even the most accessible online programs can pose challenges since not all have equal resources for students with disabilities.

ICT accessibility and employment of persons with disabilities

Unemployment is one of the biggest issues facing us today, specifically the disability community. Entering and influencing disability employment increases confidence, expands their social network and skills, and provides opportunities to develop a career by gaining new work skills and knowledge. In recent years, major developments have been made to achieve workplace equality for all persons with disabilities.

For persons with disabilities of working age, the rapid progress in (ICT) and assistive technology offers ever-increasing opportunities to participate in the world of work.

The estimated 1 billion persons with disabilities worldwide represent some 15 percent of the global population and are at higher risk of poverty than others. Persons with disabilities find it difficult to get jobs because of the inaccessibility of buildings, public transport, information, and ICT accessibility and mistaken assumptions about their capacity to work. In all countries, unemployment among women and men with disabilities is higher than those of persons without disabilities.

We know that there are challenges ahead facing people living with disabilities regarding employment. Still, the key question is: "How can hiring persons with disabilities facilitate their employment, provide them financial independence, a better standard of living, and improve their skills"?

"How can we help job seekers with disabilities by using new technologies, assistive technology tools, and ICT accessibility"?

ICT Accessible and information technology can be used by people with a wide range of abilities and disabilities. It incorporates the principles of universal design. Each user can interact with the technology in the best way. Accessible technology is either directly accessible -in other words, usable without assistive technology -or compatible with standard assistive technology. Just as buildings with ramps and elevators are accessible to wheelchair users, products that adhere to accessible design principles are usable by people with a wide range of abilities and disabilities.

The UN Convention on the Rights of Persons with Disabilities (UNCRPD) recognizes in Article 27 "the right of persons with disabilities to work, on an equal basis with others; this includes the right to the opportunity to gain a living by work freely chosen or accepted in a labor market and work environment that is open, inclusive and accessible to persons with disabilities." This includes prohibition of discrimination, protection of rights, access to education, employment in the public and private sector, possibilities for self-employment, and support to maintain employment on equal terms.

Data on persons with disabilities are hard to come by in almost every country. Specific data on their employment situation are even harder to find. Yet, persons with disabilities face the same predicament everywhere.

According to the International Labour Organization (ILO), an estimated 386 million of the world's working-age people have some kind of disability; Unemployment among persons with disabilities is as high as 80 percent in some countries. Often, employers assume that persons with disabilities are unable to work.

The role of ICT in disability and employment

Persons with disabilities can participate in the workplace like all employees; they can bring a range of skills, talents, and abilities to the workplace, and there is a range of support to help them find and keep employment.

ICT plays a vital role in the workplace; active workplace measures promote the adoption of these technologies and can improve the standard of living of persons with disabilities, promote workplace inclusiveness, and increase society's supply of labor.

United Nations published fact sheets on employment of persons with disabilities are summarized in the following:

- **Employing persons with disabilities: Fears and realities**

  Persons with disabilities are frequently not considered potential members of the workforce. Perception, fear, myth, and prejudice continue to limit understanding and acceptance of disability in workplaces everywhere. Myths abound, including that persons with disabilities are unable to work and that accommodating a person with a disability in the workplace is expensive. Contrary to these notions, many companies have found that persons with disabilities are more than capable.

- **Why hire persons with disabilities?**

  - Just like others, most persons with disabilities want a dignified and productive life.

- Employment provides income and opportunities for social participation, which is especially important for people with disabilities.
- Spending on systems and facilities for persons with disabilities is not for the privilege of a small minority but an investment for everyone.
- Diverse work groups develop better solutions to business challenges.
- Many companies have found that employing people with disabilities has improved their ability to understand and serve their customers with disabilities. Adapting services to meet the diverse needs of people with disabilities allows businesses to develop greater flexibility, build a reputation, and reach a sizeable market.

However, employment outcomes for persons with disabilities increasingly continue, where new technologies can enable workers with disabilities to be competitive in the workplace and enable those who were economically inactive in the past to enter the workplace and earn a living. Recently, the pursuit of ICT accessibility has been touted as promising. It could contribute to the development of persons with disabilities and their economic independence and, in the process, promote inclusive societies and sustainable development.

Technological change has led to the automation of tasks that were previously carried out on a labor-intensive basis, and some have lost their jobs as a result; however, it has been, on the whole, positive for persons with disabilities—particularly in information technology and assistive devices that enable them to live more independently than in the past.
The development of information technology has also enabled women and men with disabilities to work with the kind of flexibility they require.

Telecentre and Distance Learning options have now opened up, offering people with limited mobility the possibility of working and training from home or in a central location.

Barriers for persons with disabilities regarding employment

Persons with disabilities face plenty of obstacles that impede or even prevent them from being involved and participating in the workplace; the most important barriers for them are key elements of employment that can be diminished or even eliminated through technology.

The Synthesis Report of the ICT Opportunity for a Disability-Inclusive Development Framework addressed the main challenges of ICT accessibility, including enabling access to job opportunities for persons with disabilities.

The report indicates that there are many challenges to promoting the employment of persons with disabilities; attitudinal barriers are still highly prevalent in the workplace. In addition, assistive technology is expensive, policies that foster widespread availability of accessible ICTs are lacking, and policy implementation and effective implementation mechanisms are lacking. Persons with disabilities are perceived as unable to perform highly skilled jobs. This barrier creates a situation where the only jobs available for persons with disabilities are low-skilled labor.

Furthermore, Organization for Economic Co-operation and Development (OECD) research has shown that persons with disabilities are twice as likely to be unemployed all over the OECD and that, when employed, they work part-time or at reduced hours more often than others. Consequently, the purchasing power of persons with disabilities is comparatively lower than that of other groups, which in turn aggravates the issue of affordability of accessible ICTs.

ICT accessibility to increase access to work opportunities

ICT is one of the central drivers of productivity and success for all workers in today's workplace. However, when workplace technology is not accessible to those with disabilities, it excludes and becomes a barrier to success and career advancement. It limits opportunities for persons with disabilities to get hired or to excel in a position when they are unable to perform their job duties because they can't access basic workplace tools.

ICT accessibility is the next frontier of the accessibility movement and a gateway to a more productive and inclusive workforce.

Some have global reach and have been harmonized across national boundaries to help ICT companies improve their accessibility. Standards and guidelines usually cover specific technologies; the most well-known is the family of guidelines for web technologies produced by the World Wide Web Consortium's (W3C) Web Accessibility Initiative (WAI). All technologies should be usable by as many people as possible. To advance the employment of persons with disabilities, we should promote the development and adoption of accessible workplace technology that can be used effectively by all disabled employees.

Many assistive technology solutions can assist in a variety of occupations and workplaces! Application programs such as screen readers can enable persons with blind and visual impairments to access job vacancies. People with motor disabilities can use assistive technologies such as special keyboards or eye-tracking software, voice recognition, used instead of a mouse or keyboard; alternative input devices that enable control of computers through means other than a standard keyboard or mouse (e.g., head-operated pointing devices and "sip and puff" systems controlled by breathing). Other new technologies replacing physical activity with automated production of goods or performance of demanding tasks have opened up many employment opportunities for women and men with disabilities, and other new assistive devices help persons with disabilities perform jobs that were previously out of reach.

Indirectly, assistive devices also facilitate them getting ready to work in a good environment.

A 2013 report by the Global Initiative for Inclusive ICTs (G3ict) on measuring progress based on ICT accessibility in compliance with the UN Convention on the Rights of Persons with Disabilities (CRPD) showed a deficit in making essential services accessible to persons with disabilities in countries that have ratified CRPD.

Persons with disabilities; capability and value-added workplace

Persons with disabilities have skills, abilities, and experience that can add value to the workplace. Make workplaces accessible, search for talented employees with disabilities, and find the right person for the job.

An accessible workplace will maximize productivity by eliminating barriers that can prevent persons with disabilities from working to their potential.

ICT adjustments include any information communication technology changes made to ensure you have equal access to participate in the workplace. Accessibility features can benefit everyone, not just those with a disability.

Below are just a few examples of assistive technology and programs for creating accessible workplaces:

- Computer-based screen magnifiers and ZoomText
- Voice recognition software
- Screen readers for phones
- Text-to-speech (TTS)
- Dictation software
- Alternative keyboards
- CCTV systems and video magnifiers
- Optical low-vision aids
- Braille production system, Braille reader, Braille typewriters
- DAISY books and applications to create DAISY documents
- A telephone typewriter (TTY) and captioned telephone
- A permanent microphone stand, earpiece holder, wired microphone, and a wireless microphone to operate the computer
- The Microsoft accessibility tool Sticky Keys
- Listening devices, audio format and tools, teleconferences, and voicemail
- keyboard stands, accessible desks, document holders to make typing easier, and office printers
- An environmental control unit with programmable infrared control for operating devices using infrared remotes to use the voice recognition software for computers to operate by voice command.
- Communication devices such as hands-free telephones
- Adjust the height of shared items such as photocopiers, printers, and fax machines to promote ease of access and reach.

The Partnership on Employment & Accessible Technology (PEAT) pointed out some guidelines to help employers work with their (ICT) vendors and internal developers, standards, laws, regulations, common accessibility standards, and, most importantly, technical standards to consider for workplaces.

The Australian Government Initiative, National Disability Coordination Officer (NDCO), was released in 2014. The booklet provides information about technology that can be used in the workplace by people with disabilities.

Finally:

Equal Access to Employment for All: Persons with disabilities are important in making a positive workplace contribution. It is generally found that a person with a disability develops into a well-adjusted, productive worker in an atmosphere of acceptance, cooperation, and goodwill. It is often seen that workers with disabilities are more productive than their co-workers, that they are less absent from work, and that they show great loyalty towards their company.

Employment is key to combating poverty and achieving social inclusion and participation for all working-age persons.

The low employment levels among persons with disabilities, specifically in developing countries, are a major factor in the economic and social disparities.

Many issues affect the capacity of persons with disabilities to obtain employment and to be able to progress in their jobs.

Barriers to education, lack of reasonable accommodation, lack of accessibility to infrastructures and information, limitations related to legal capacity, as well as attitudinal barriers in society are some of the areas that have a significant impact on the employment of persons with disabilities but with the advent of ICT and technological advances removed many obstacles for persons with disabilities in their aspirations to pursue the careers of their choice.

Tourism destinations and accessibility for persons with disabilities

Studies about the tourism experience of persons with disabilities first arose in the late 1970s, and even in the late 1980s and early 1990s, researchers only "toyed with this subject" (McKercher et al., 2003). Nowadays, growing studies are concentrating on the tourist experience of persons with disabilities. Recent studies highlight the need for further investigation into the travel experiences of persons with disabilities, and other studies also highlight the accessibility issues.

Accessible tourism is largely encouraged to make it easy for everyone to enjoy tourism experiences (Darcy & Dickson, 2009). The fundamental principle is captured within the view of human rights, the United Nations Convention on the Rights of People with Disabilities, 2006, is steered by the following principles: dignity, independence, full and effective participation, reverence, and recognition of disability as part of human variety and parity of opportunity.

Tourism for people with disabilities means using the general and basic mainstreaming framework to ensure access to the physical environment, the transportation system, information and communications channels, and a wide range of public facilities and services.

Tourism destinations should be made disability-friendly through regulations, monitoring, and supervision of accessibility, structures, and the environment. Today, tourism is an integral part of many people's lifestyles.

Research has found that the participation of persons with disabilities in tourism is limited due to many factors, such as the inaccessible tourism environment, the nature of transport services, the language barrier, and the lack of tourism awareness towards persons with disabilities.

Accessible tourism is a very big market. And, as the population ages, it will get even bigger. By 2020, on some estimates, 25 % of travel and leisure spending will come from people who have some form of disability. There is also a multiplier effect here: people who are elderly or who have a disability often take other people along when they are traveling. Accessible tourism is a very big market that is bringing growth and jobs. Investing in it can open up a market of millions of persons with disabilities worldwide. "Accessible Tourism in Europe".

Accordingly, tourism should be accessible to all travelers. Accessible tourism ensures that tourist destinations, products, and services are accessible to all people, regardless of their physical limitations, disabilities, or age. Facilitating travel for persons with disabilities is a basic, cross-cutting, and integral element of any responsible and sustainable tourism policy. The tourism industry will recognize that persons with disabilities have equal rights to tourism services and opportunities: independent travel, accessible facilities, trained staff, reliable information, and inclusive marketing. See "Recommendations on Accessible Tourism", World Tourism Organization (UNWTO).

In this context, accessible tourism for all is not only about providing access to persons with disabilities but also addresses the creation of universally designed environments that can support people with temporary disabilities.

UNWTO indicated recommendations on the appropriate measures to ensure that persons with disabilities have equal access to the physical environment, transportation, information, and communications, including computer systems, information and communications technology, and other services and facilities open to the public or for public use in urban areas as well as rural and coastal zones.

Accessibility must be present throughout the tourism chain, and the links between all sites, services, and activities must be well-planned and tested. Elements of the tourism chain include Tourism destination management, tourism information and advertising, urban and architectural environments, modes of transport and stations, accommodation, food service, conventions, cultural activities, and other tourism activities and events.

In an increasingly globalized world, an awareness of the need to factor accessible tourism into decision-making and policies needs significant attention. Government and other stakeholders must be encouraged to prioritize the sector's positive effects and find ways to mitigate the detrimental impacts. Therefore, an urgent need is to inform policymakers about appropriate interventions to access tourism for persons with disabilities. For example, in Australia, Tourism

Victoria's Accessible Tourism Plan outlines strategies and actions to help the industry meet these obligations and then go further to cater to all people with access requirements by:

- Increasing industry awareness and understanding of the accessibility needs of tourists
- Encouraging new and existing products to capitalize on the benefits of providing accessible tourism.
- Disseminating information on accessible tourism products and attractions.

Persons with disability have a right to enjoy travel leisure experiences; accessibility and participation in tourism will enhance social inclusion, but transportation constraints, inaccessible accommodation and tourism sites, and inadequate customer services still characterize their travel experiences. Suppose tourism industry professionals are to succeed in accessing these potential new markets. In that case, they must understand the needs of the tourism industry and learn how to respond to these challenges to benefit the tourism industry and persons with disabilities.

The studies of the UN-ESCAP Barrier-Free Tourism for People with Disabilities in the Asian and Pacific Region have shown the major issues about challenges such as travel planning and information for persons with disabilities; one issue is the need for a shared understanding of what constitutes access and disability by the stakeholders (people with disabilities; operators; tourism sectors; intermediaries), also transport barriers, transport options are not available for easy use by people with disabilities in addition the lack of accessible accommodation, one travel planning information issue is obtaining information about barrier-free accommodation. Many accommodation operators do not understand what accessible or barrier-free accommodation entails. They are often unable to provide accurate or detailed information about the features of their rooms. In many cases, accommodation operators represent their rooms as accessible or barrier-free, but people with disabilities find the rooms unsuitable.

Many older people, families, and persons with disabilities are keen to travel. Still, wide variation in the level of access within destinations, combined with poor information and negative experiences, discourages potential customers.

The demand for universally accessible tourism products needs to be addressed urgently. It would be prudent for the tourism service providers to consider the merits of accelerating measures to address the needs of this sector of the market based on the predicted demand, which far exceeds the current availability of Universal Accessible accommodation, services, and facilities. Improved accessibility will benefit the tourism industry economically and assist overall social integration. Universal Accessibility would be greatly enhanced by up-scaling service delivery in all the critical touch points such as the following: Access to information, accessibility on the Web, ICT accessibility has a major part to play in barrier-free tourism., communication, accommodation, accessibility training, staff training is vital to the promotion of truly accessible tourism and Design for All.

Also, other factors are conditioning the tourist's accessibility to one destination that can be resumed as a Barrier-free destination: "infrastructures and facilities," transport by "air, land, and sea, suitable for all users," high-quality services, and marketing.

The improvement of accessibility of tourist products and services, using global solutions based especially on the principle of "Design for All," will be a requirement of the present and future tourists towards the tourist sector, and cooperation between the public and private sectors must be at the heart of accessible tourism.

Applying accessible telecentre for refugees with disabilities

"Let us bravely move forward to give this new idea its place in our hearts and minds."

Refugees and displaced persons living with disabilities are amongst the most isolated, socially excluded, and marginalized of all displaced populations.

Some refugees and displaced persons may have lived their whole lives with a disability, and others may have become disabled during the conflict or natural disaster that led to their flight. They are" Too often invisible and forgotten."

For refugees with disabilities and their families who have fled the conflict in their country, living with physical and mental disabilities poses huge day-to-day challenges. Still, we can look out to a brighter future to support them.

"Conflict has the right to psychological recovery and social integration. Therefore, psychosocial programs for children in war-affected areas that fail to reach disabled children fail. This should be the prerogative of organizations and institutions when they plan, monitor, and evaluate psychosocial interventions" (United Nations, 2006).

All persons with disabilities who live in conflict-affected areas have the same rights support, as enshrined in the Convention on the Rights of Persons with Disabilities (CRPD). However, persons with disabilities are often overlooked in psychosocial programs. See more about (UN-Rights of Refugees with Disabilities)

In refugee situations, persons with disabilities are particularly vulnerable. Without independent mobility, families fleeing danger may be forced to abandon them, exposing persons with disabilities to more health and safety risks and reducing their chances of survival. For those who may manage to reach refugee camps, the situation in the camps gives rise to an increase in cases of impairment through poor nutrition and health conditions, injuries relating to conflict, accidents, burns, torture, and trauma.

It is recommended that States and UNHCR, as applicable, ensure that refugee status determination and all other relevant procedures are accessible and designed to enable persons with disabilities to fully and fairly represent their claims with the necessary support. See more (the UNHCR guidance on Working with Persons with disabilities in Forced Displacement, 2011)

Emergency arrangements typically fail to address the specific needs of persons with disabilities, either in buildings or in the provision of essential social assistance. Their existence and needs are rarely acknowledged. In the daily running of the refugee camps, they are often the last to receive care and access to fundamental services; lack of education, personal care needs, and communication difficulties add to their problems.

Many refugees with disabilities may need accessibility materials and other facilities services, including rehabilitation care and counseling, general public awareness campaigns, and promotion activities for mainstreaming disability issues into all sectors in the camps. Specifically, women and children with disabilities are often exposed to sexual violence in refugee camps and physical assault, exploitation, and neglect. They are excluded from education and lack the support to help them develop to their full capacity.

"Building the capacity of communities in this way has a positive impact in terms of the inclusion of disability issues in the refugee camps."

Telecentre to support refugees with disabilities

Together, we can create a welcoming environment to fortify capacity and compassionately for refugees, displaced persons, and their families who have fled the conflict in their country. We can provide them protection, advocacy, education, health, and other services. There are big challenges for persons with disabilities in refugee camps, including:

- Lack of visibility: In general, refugees with disabilities are rarely acknowledged. They are not given a chance to be heard. Their existence is seldom acknowledged, and for them to benefit from education, communications, awareness, health, and nutrition programs, these programs need to address the needs of persons with disabilities.

- Disability awareness: Those who manage refugee situations have little knowledge, skills, and understanding of disability. Therefore, camps and buildings are designed without considering Universal Design (UD) and accessibility services. Personal care regarding mobility and communication gadgets, aids, and adaptations is also not considered.

- Communication: Supervisors and educators in communications skills at the refugee camps are not educated or empowered to communicate in sign language or Braille and find it extremely hard to interact with persons with disabilities.

Refugees with disabilities lack awareness of their rights; many of them are not aware of their rights and are, therefore, unable to demand these rights.

What can we do to help?

Providing accessible access to services, facilities, and accessible educational programs for refugees with disabilities may make them eligible for accommodations that can help them teach and promote their communication skills.

The research found that accessible inclusion could be a good entry point for refugees with disabilities. For example, through early intervention programs, refugee children and women with disabilities could be referred to appropriate health services, and parent support groups were a positive starting point for providing psychosocial support to their parents.

Today, there is a need to organize training sessions on accessibility issues such as awareness sessions, encourage the members of the communities in the camps to take care of persons with disabilities; there is a need to raise the awareness of other NGOs to organizations work, and also to enable them to include disability in their projects for example, building accessible telecentres in refugees camps.

Another important part of the telecentres is supplying refugees with disabilities with assistive devices, such as walking, toileting, and standing aids. They should also train families to use these specific devices, including different approaches to environmental issues.

The fact that refugees are settled in emergencies means that little thought is given to refugees with disabilities in the camps.

Benefits of ICT Accessibility in Refugee Camps

- ICT accessibility has become an essential tool for humanitarian aid work and its role in education and healthcare, particularly in educating large groups of refugees with disabilities from diverse backgrounds and with varying levels of basic education and literacy.

- Accessibility finds innovative use of ICT in education, particularly within humanitarian work's harsh and volatile environment.

- ICT accessibility provides a learning opportunity for refugees with disabilities.

- ICTs provide an important space to help refugees with disabilities regain autonomy and lead as normal a life as possible while in displacement.

- The use of ICT accessibility and portable devices has allowed refugees with disabilities to obtain skills and education in a safe and secure environment.
- Persons with disabilities and children with disabilities must be considered a key target group across all intervention processes from identification, assessment, planning, delivery of support programs, monitoring, and evaluation.

What do we need, and how could the plan work?

- Advocate for change globally with donors, policymakers, and humanitarian workers to inform advocacy campaigns focused on improving access to services for persons with disabilities in crisis-affected areas worldwide.
- Support the voice of refugees with disabilities. Refugees and displaced persons with disabilities seek to facilitate their participation and voice in all activities. Examples of such approaches include facilitating activities with refugees to formulate ideas for change, which they can present to organizations and stakeholders in workshops, and bridging the gap between persons with disabilities and the implementers of refugee programs.

To increase the participation of refugees with disabilities:

- Ensure the importance of pedagogical support, usually missing in ICT intensive training in developing country contexts. A low-tech ICT approach is appropriate, using local knowledge constructions in refugee camp environments to disseminate education, health, and environmental knowledge effectively.
- Ensure that refugees with disabilities are included in accessibility programs during or after conflict situations, and minimize the stress on the person with disability and their relatives.

There are two recommendations listed below:

Local organizations of persons with disabilities and parents of children with disabilities, together with non-governmental organizations (NGOs) working in the field of disability, should be involved and consulted by humanitarian agencies to ensure the needs of persons with disabilities are recognized.

Action and care are needed by humanitarian aid agencies to proactively seek out persons with disabilities to ensure they are registered and supported in a humanitarian situation, as they are often hidden away and not easy to identify.

Refugees with disabilities are "forgotten," "vulnerable," and "invisible." It's time today to work together to support them!

Library services and accessibility of eBooks for persons with disabilities

"Make more books accessible for your library; you do not have to be an expert in technology or accessibility to make a very useful contribution in your library and to readers with disabilities."

To make a library accessible, you need social and economic resources. Many improvements can be implemented with little money—or possibly without cost. The solution can often be found through a change in staff attitude and new thinking.

Everyone, including people with disabilities, can access library services and materials to meet their information, inspiration, education, and recreation needs.

Every person with a disability has the right to be treated with the same dignity, consistency, and consideration as any member of the general public who receives library service.

The library is increasingly important in ensuring that all persons with disabilities can access the Internet and other information resources using assistive technology, network technologies, and ICT accessibility.

We need to emphasize the principle of normalization, inclusion, and integration of Persons with Disabilities into mainstream community life.

Assure library standards for Persons with Disabilities by collection development, promotion, and delivery of services, computer applications, and adaptive technology for making electronic resources accessible.

Universal design principles should be incorporated into every library policy regarding library services for People with Disabilities. Library policies will be applied in a way that considers the needs of people with disabilities and respects the principles of dignity, independence, and integration.

Addressing library services for persons with disabilities

All library materials should ideally be accessible to all persons with disabilities. There are various ways to achieve this goal.

Libraries should acquire talking (books, newspapers, periodicals), video/DVD books with subtitles and sign language, Braille books, large print books, accessible e-books, easy-to-read books, tactile picture books, or other non-print materials.

- Improve and facilitate access to alternative-format library materials for Persons with Disabilities.
- Collections of alternative-format library materials for readers with disabilities
- Exploring ways to create and improve library services and resources for people with print disabilities.
- Facilitate information exchange resource-sharing among libraries serving Persons with Disabilities and meet their changing needs.
- Providing information and expertise to the general community and organizations about providing library services to Persons with Disabilities.

Library services for people with print disabilities

The library needs of people with print disabilities are generally the same as those of sighted people. However, by definition, people with print disabilities cannot use conventional print materials. They must depend upon large type, audio (spoken word), tactile devices (such as Braille), and mechanical or optical aids - or a combination.

Collections for people with print disabilities should include:

- Talking books, audio magazines, and newspapers;
- Audio tape, CD/DVD, or in DAISY format;
- Large-print books;
- Computer files of text;
- Braille and other tactile materials;
- Audio-descriptive videos.

Providing equipment to facilitate the use of 'special-format' and standard-print materials will benefit people with print disabilities the most.

Libraries should consider acquiring or facilitating access to the following:

- Illuminated CCTVs (magnifiers using a television screen to display prints of varying sizes and contrasts).

- Microfiche enlargers (magnifiers using a television screen to display enlarged microfiche).

Other equipment that could be considered for inclusion in libraries include Voice-output devices, Optical Character Recognition (OCR) devices, Braille-output devices, Braille printers with voice output, large print, Versabrailles, and Typewriters.

Library services for people with deaf or hearing-impaired

A basic collection of materials in formats that are readily accessible to the deaf and hearing impaired, so we need to develop services to assist them; the primary goal of any specialized program for the deaf and hearing impaired must be to provide equal access to all programs and services that are enjoyed by the library's hearing clientele.

- Books and pamphlets on sign language, dictionaries of signs;
- High-interest/low-vocabulary reading materials;
- DVDs contain sub-titles as a standard feature and illustrated materials;
- Films and videos, including closing caption video;
- Loop system, audio loop, and counter loop;
- Telecommunication devices (TDD/TTY).

Library services for cognitive disabilities

People who are cognitively delayed may need types of support. Planning for libraries can often include individuals with cognitive disabilities because many function fairly well. They have preferences and can articulate them, and they can give insight into the problems they have in using a library. Every library should provide a basic collection covering a broad range of information as an integral part of the library collection. People with cognitive and intellectual disabilities will benefit from access to:

- Books in enlarged print;
- High-interest, low-vocabulary materials and books;
- Books on tape-and-text kits;
- Illustrated materials (Picture books), audio materials, and music collections;
- Spoken-word collections;

- Audio and videotape in Daisy format.

Library services for persons with physical disabilities

Persons with physical disabilities may need assistance doing physical tasks using the library.

They need access to computers for reading at the library with the following Software:

- Voice recognition;
- Word prediction;
- Screen enlargement;
- Software for converting print documents;
- Scan and read programs;
- Text highlighting and advanced reading in different formats.

Electronic Books

E-books are an extremely popular topic these days. E-books are an especially exciting development for readers with disabilities because their properties make them ideal for finding alternative access forms.

When an e-book is presented in an accessible format on an accessible e-book reader, the user can choose to read the book using text-to-speech, Braille, or magnification. Furthermore, accessible e-books in an open market benefit everyone.

For persons with disabilities, their needs can be fulfilled simply with a large print or an existing PDF version. In contrast, others find a fully navigable structured file such as a DAISY file, an EPUB 3 file, or an HTML-based e-book that they can use with text-to-speech software essential. Other blind readers prefer Braille, which can be used as a standard embossed edition or as an electronic publication accessible through a refreshable Braille device.

Creating files with different formats

It is worth noting that even the most "accessible" formats can be misused to create wholly inaccessible books. The potential for accessibility is built into the format but must be correctly and sensitively used to produce an accessible product. This is true with all formats; built-in accessibility cannot be assumed. It is hugely beneficial to conduct user testing "accessible" content to ensure these files are correctly produced.

The publishing industry uses many different file formats, which vary in the degree to which they are "accessible."

No file format is automatically accessible; it is possible to produce inaccessible publications in any format for most purposes.

Here are different formats to get started with understanding eBook accessibility.

Microsoft Word Document Format (DOC)

Microsoft Word: For many print-impaired readers, particularly in the education sector, this file format offers the easiest route to accessible information. The file's text content is easily mutable and can contain all three elements of structure, content, and appearance. Creating a useful file in Word may mean creating a new one at the end of the production process.

Portable Document Format (PDF)

- **Print-ready PDFs:** These are often the least accessible file formats. They contain content and appearance but only minimally reflect structure; there is no reading order or structural or semantic tagging. This particularly applies to image-based PDFs (e.g., scans of text or graphically rich books), as they contain no textual content. If PDFs are used, they should be edited in Adobe Acrobat to ensure the underlying text is present and to add tagging.

- **PDFs optimized for digital use:** These files tend to be more navigable and include structure, so for some users, they may provide a reasonable option. They can consist of a reading order, ALT tags, etc. These files have all three elements: structure, content, and appearance. However, in most circumstances, they tend not to be as customizable for individual reader needs as other formats and should not be seen as the format of choice.

Digital Accessible Information Systems (DAISY) Format

This has become the foremost standard specialist format for creating accessible versions for the print impaired. It can be the most accessible file format available.

It is essentially an XML-based e-book format created by the DAISY Consortium, representing libraries for people with print disabilities.

A DAISY book can be explained as a package of digital files that may include one or more digital audio files containing a human or pre-recorded synthesized narration of part or all of the source text; a marked-up file containing some or all of the text; a synchronization file to relate markings in the text file with time points in the audio file; and a navigation control file which enables the user to move smoothly between files while synchronization between text and audio is maintained. Specialist DAISY players can play the audio, read the text using Text to Speech, and navigate the book flexibly. The DAISY Standard allows the producer full flexibility regarding the mix of text and audio, ranging from audio-only to full text and audio to text-only. The DAISY Consortium offers an open suite of software tools, "The DAISY Pipeline," designed to assist in creating DAISY files, which also has increasing support for conversion to EPUB 3.

Electronic Publication (EPUB) Format

This is rapidly becoming the universal "e-book" format for commercial publishers. As version EPUB 3 becomes more widely available, it is increasingly seen as the most suitable format for commercial exploitation and meeting accessibility needs.

EPUB is an open standard for e-book creation and distribution and is the most common file format for commercially available e-books. It can be "read" on almost all e-reader devices (except Amazon's Kindle – and even there, most Amazon Kindle books start life as EPUBs and are converted to the Kindle format before distribution).

The latest version, EPUB 3, combines HTML's ease of creation and expressive capability with a host of accessibility options. The DAISY Consortium has adopted it as its next-generation digital standard delivery format to replace the specialist DAISY format.

For publishers, the same file format used to deliver mainstream commercial e-books can also provide optimum accessibility to print-impaired readers. It is constructed using ordinary HTML5 and CSS (cascading style sheets), so publishers are familiar with the basic technology, and a rich set of authoring and production tools is available. On top of this, EPUB 3 defines a range of features that improve navigation and accessibility, such as detailed structural markup and the ability to include pre-recorded speech synchronized with the text (called 'media overlays). EPUB 3 allows accessible video, mathematical and technical content (via MathML), and interactivity. Using EPUB 3, publishers can make their mainstream commercial products highly accessible.

Hyper Text Markup Language (HTML) Format

These files can be among the most accessible on the market. Using the predominant Web technology, we can ensure that customers with disabilities will be well-practiced in using the file type with their assistive technology. Customization within Web browsers is simple and well-known. As these books are played in web browsers, working on these files makes them highly flexible and will benefit a wide audience, including users without disabilities. Also, customizations users have already set up to access the Web will likely carry over this eBook directly. Some versions of HTML e-books can incorporate MathML, providing access to maths and sciences to persons with disabilities.

Extensible Markup Language (XML) Format

More specifically, all types of XML files that logically tag book files (using a proprietary or a standard DTD (document type definition) or schema, such as DocBook) have the potential to be extremely accessible. They contain structure and content but not appearance. However, end users (and those who support them) are unlikely to have the specialized XML skills needed to use them. Hence, these files are likely only suitable when dealing with people with unusually advanced technical capabilities, technically skilled commercial organizations, or intermediary organizations supporting Persons with Disabilities.

These XML files are normally transformed into a distribution format, such as EPUB 3 or DAISY.

Layout Application Files

These files can contain structure, content, and appearance in a mutable form. In contrast to Word files, they represent the "final version" of a publication, as no editing takes place afterward; they could be useful for the provision of content in a "professional" or mediated context, such as providing publisher content to an e-book distributor like CourseSmart as eTextbooks. However, typical print-impaired readers have no access to or skill in using applications such as Adobe InDesign, Adobe Illustrator, or QuarkXPress; in general, application files are unsuitable for provision to those seeking accessible formats. However, InDesign V 6 already has an export option to EPUB 3; Adobe has indicated that InDesign V 7's "Export to EPUB" can be further improved.

LaTeX Files

LaTeX is a high-quality typesetting system; it includes features designed to produce technical and scientific documentation. LaTeX files can sometimes be suitable, particularly for mathematical and technical material.

Publishers who receive manuscripts in TeX or LaTeX or use these formats in their typesetting process may be able to supply the files in this format for accessibility purposes. However, they are suitable only for print-impaired readers who have the necessary technical skills (or access to them).

Library staff and training to support persons with disabilities

Accessibility to the library should be a clearly defined management responsibility. All staff must be knowledgeable about various types of disabilities and how to assist them best. A designated employee should act as a liaison with a disability reader.

How to train staff?

Examples of appropriate staff training include:

- Staff training and raising awareness about disabilities issues.
- Staff need to be aware of current terminology relating to disabilities and understand that the person comes before their disability.

- Staff need to be educated about the abilities and realistic limitations of Persons with Disabilities.
- Invite persons with disabilities to staff meetings to talk about their needs as library users.
- Distribute emails and other information about library services to specific groups of disabilities to staff regularly.
- Assisted staff in developing appropriate communication skills and provided them with the necessary collection development skills.

Finally:

Libraries play a vital role in the lives of persons with disabilities by facilitating their full participation in society.

Libraries should use strategies based on the principles of universal design to ensure that library policy, resources, and services meet the needs of all people.

We need to plan technological solutions and access points, for example (telecentre), based on the concepts of universal design, which are essential for the effective use of information and other library services by all people. Libraries should work with Persons with Disabilities, local communities, organizations, and vendors to integrate assistive technology into their facilities and services to meet the needs of people with a broad range of disabilities, including learning, mobility, sensory, and developmental disabilities.

Library staff should be aware of how available technologies address disabilities and know how to assist all users with library technology.

Accessibility to strengthen arts and culture for persons with disabilities

Art is a visual language that provides another means of communication; since the earliest civilizations, art has become an integral part of society. Today, art plays a major role in society.

Art provides opportunities to solve problems, observe, and strengthen aesthetic awareness and critical thinking (likes and dislikes). Try to imagine a society without the humanizing influence of the arts. You will have to strip out most of what is pleasurable in life and much that is educationally critical and socially essential. Life without the collective resources of our libraries, museums, theatres, and galleries, or the personal expression of literature, music, and art, would be static and sterile – no creative arguments about the past, no diverse and stimulating present, and no dreams of the future.

Art seeks to please people with beauty. In a broken world, sometimes it is important to allow persons with disabilities to realize that there is still beauty. Hence, art can refresh people and remind them of better things or transcendent realities.

One way to empower all persons with disabilities is by educating ourselves to learn how to provide and model best practices for accommodating and improving accessibility to learning and participating in the rich visual language of art.

The openness of art instruction (many solutions, not single answers) naturally allows the expressions or voices of multiple learners. There is a need to increase and learn that persons with disabilities have the opportunity to be self-expressive and successful in an artistic medium, which can often diffuse or transcend the sense of isolation and frustration they may feel when working with their disability in daily life.

Persons with disabilities can express and communicate their thoughts via paintings, sculptures, songs, and other art forms. Many of them struggle to communicate their thoughts and feelings. They may have trouble finding the words or using language effectively. The visual arts, such as painting, drawing, music, and computer graphics, can give them a non-verbal way to express themselves and interact with others; for example, graphics and design inspiration programs using ICT tools and accessibility can provide alternative avenues for creative expression.

They are learning to express themselves through art and often feel that the essence of who they are is trapped inside their bodies. Persons with disabilities with art can express important values within that society to people in memorable ways; art can be used to reinforce values and even bring people together with private and public sectors to seek innovative ways to employ the arts for persons with disabilities to improve and strengthen communities, interest in assessing the impact of their artworks, arts advocates and researchers could make a variety of ambitious claims about how the arts impact communities.

Accordingly, we must raise awareness among the public across the cultural, educational, and political sectors. Among those who influence investment in both the public and private sectors, we will, in time, articulate a new language of cultural value that will help persons with disabilities to understand the essentials of arts and make their lives in full color.

Accessibility and the arts for inspiring creativity

Today's technologies offer multiple ways to assist persons with disabilities in expressing their ideas, aspirations, and creativity through art.

How can someone paint a picture if she cannot hold a paintbrush?

How can someone create in clay when he cannot touch it?

How can someone draw when the drawing tools are inaccessible due to size or shape?

ICT accessibility can help people with disabilities create independently and translate their thoughts through art.

With art specialists, they can creatively adapt art and participate in meaningful art-making with their peers. Improving the arts and ICT accessibility can make the arts accessible to them.

Accessibility, ICT accessibility, and Assistive Technology work to achieve goals, such as Providing technical assistance to open existing programs and make the arts fully accessible to persons with disabilities.

We are all looking forward to diversity and inclusion; We want diversity that includes disability. Inclusive access will enable persons with disabilities to participate fully at all levels in the arts, and it is vital to have an arts and cultural environment that reflects the full diversity of life.

ICT accessibility in the education of children with Down syndrome

Down syndrome (Trisomy 21) is the world's most common chromosomal disorder and cause of intellectual disability. It is not an illness or disease and occurs at conception. It occurs in one of every 1,000 to 1 in 1,100 live births worldwide, and each year, approximately 3,000 to 5,000 children are born with this chromosome disorder" (WHO).

Down syndrome affects but does not determine development. Persons with Down syndrome are unique in their talents, abilities, thoughts, and interests.

Everyone with Down syndrome will experience some delay in all areas of their development and some degree of learning disability. This will, however, vary significantly from individual to individual. What happens after birth will be far more important in shaping the outlook for any individual with Down syndrome than the presence of an extra chromosome.

Research provided a clear picture of the specific profile of learning needs of children with Down syndrome, specifically when targeted early intervention.

Research suggested that children with Down syndrome do better, across a range of academic and other measures, in inclusive mainstream settings rather than segregated settings, irrespective of their level of learning ability.

Research has shown that children and young people with Down syndrome not only take longer to learn new skills but also learn differently in some key areas, benefiting from some teaching strategies that are different from those typically used in education. These include approaches to number skills, reading, and speech and language skills.

Children with Down syndrome can do better despite slowly progressing in various areas of development, including gross and fine motor skills, personal and social development, communication, cognition, and self-help. The syndrome's impact on development varies across developmental areas. This is described as a specific profile associated with the condition or a pattern of strengths and weaknesses.

The extent of delays is not the same across all areas, and there are significant differences between individuals. The development of individuals with Down syndrome is influenced by family, environment, cultural, and social factors in much the same way as everyone else.

Every learner with Down syndrome will demonstrate individual abilities, strengths, and weaknesses and have their learning characteristics. For this reason, while we can outline various factors associated with Down syndrome learners, this material should act only as background information when dealing with individual students. The temptation to generalize based on the label 'Down syndrome' should be resisted.

Member States acknowledged last year's High-level General Assembly Meeting on Disability and Development and is in line with the UN Convention on the Rights of Persons with Disabilities, which reaffirms that such persons, including those with Down syndrome, are entitled to human rights equally with others.

"The emerging post-2015 global development agenda offers a vital opportunity to build a life of dignity for all".

Training for children with Down syndrome

Children with Down's syndrome learn best from what they see and do, and the most important period for learning must be the early years. Breaking down skills at this point to gain reading, numeracy, and social skills means breaking down even the pre-reading and pre-number skills and presenting tasks that will help develop the problems with short-term memory. Training should include information about the following:

- The learning profile and the speech, language, and communication profile associated with Down syndrome;
- Inclusion issues and effective deployment of additional support, including Teaching Assistants;
- Differentiation and curriculum mapping, including levels where relevant to children with DS;
- Behavior management, including functional behavior analysis;
- Speech, language, and communication skills, and strategies to promote the development of teaching reading using visual (whole word recognition) as well as phonic approaches and understanding how to use literacy to develop spoken language; in additional number skills development including implementation of visual resources.

The research base supports recommended approaches and provides an overview of changing attitudes towards and opportunities for people with Down syndrome.

Benefits of ICT to support learning

ICT accessibility and specialist IT programs are used as tools, and learning skills are promoted to achieve training for children with Down syndrome.

ICT plays a vital role in early intervention and education services in defining the specific needs of children and young people with Down syndrome. It can develop good skills in ICT, and these technologies can support individuals in overcoming challenges faced when using other digital media. Throughout their education, trainers should participate in targeted learning activities, develop skills in using assistive technology and IT programs, and consider individual learning needs and practical application of these skills in everyday life, currently and in adulthood. Schools will require appropriate software for the individual, following individual assessment.

The lack of full and equal participation of those with Down syndrome affects not only individuals and their families but society at large.

Children with DS need relevant software to support their learning. They will need daily access to computers in accessible institutions or classrooms, with seating and workstations appropriate for the individual. Allocating a laptop to the individual may be necessary.

Computer-assisted learning and ICT specialists should consider the specific learning profile for hearing, short-term auditory, empathetic, social, working memory, speech and language, strong visual learning skills, visual difficulties, and short concentration span.

- ICT can be integrated into teaching situations at home and at school and support early cognitive development
- Using ICT helps children with DS achieve a greater level of independence in their lives, a greater autonomy at home and leisure
- Using ICT improves their opportunities for socializing
- ICT helps to improve behavior by combating boredom, decreasing frustration, and promoting success
- ICT can offer the chance for repeated success and errorless learning

- ICT plays a vital role in breaking barriers and isolation; young with DS can be involved in community activities using appropriate social media, for example.

Computer-based learning

Computer learning works best when teachers or parents are involved, monitoring progress, discussing activities, and teaching children how to use ICT accessibility and software properly. Computer-assisted learning offers particular benefits for children with Down syndrome, such as visual presentation, self-paced learning, highly motivating graphics and sound, immediate feedback, and the opportunity to control their learning.

Computer-based learning is particularly suitable for children and young with Down syndrome for several reasons:

- Suits visual learners
- Allows for non-verbal and non-written responding
- Allows learners to be in control and move at their own pace
- Provides immediate feedback
- Allows for practice and repetition of basic skills in a fun way
- It offers fun and enjoyment, very motivating
- Errorless learning – learners do not fail but are supported to succeed
- Assistive technology can be used to adapt computers and activities for almost any level of ability

(Based on M. Wood (2004) Supporting Learning and Development with ICT), Down syndrome Ireland .

Several benefits of computer-assisted learning for people with Down syndrome have been suggested by a variety of authors (Down syndrome Education Online)

Improving motivation: Pictures, sounds, and animation enhance the learning experience, which may increase a child's interest and attention.

Multi-sensory experience: computers provide both visual and auditory input. Children with Down syndrome are 'visual learners' who learn best when information is presented visually and find learning from listening more difficult. ICT is particularly well suited to this learning style. Nonverbal mode of response: Children can give nonverbal responses, demonstrating their understanding without producing a spoken response. This may be particularly difficult for them due to troubles with articulation, word finding, and intelligibility. Being in control: Children understand that they can affect their surroundings through' cause and effect' software. This sense of control develops further as children use familiar programs unassisted. Self-esteem grows as they become more independent in their learning and presentation improves.

Immediate feedback: Children are rewarded for their success immediately, e.g., with pictures, sound effects, or music, or prompted if they need to try again. The computer never gets impatient or frustrated by repeated errors; feedback is non-threatening and non-judgmental.

Errorless learning: Software can be designed to support the child in achieving repeated success. The child is supported at each step as necessary before making a mistake, allowing the child to learn a sequence of steps to achieve success every time.

Practice opportunities: Children with Down syndrome need much more practice to acquire new skills, and ICT can provide as many opportunities as necessary to achieve the same objective in the same way.

Self-paced learning: The child can proceed as fast or slow as they wish; the computer will 'wait' for the child to respond without prompting them before they have had time to process the information and construct their response fully.

Clutter-free working environment: Computer programs can provide a highly organized and predictable working environment that focuses the child on specific targets.

Assistive technology: Both hardware and software can be modified and customized to meet children's needs.

Differentiation: The Internet offers a wide range of software that can be purchased or downloaded to produce differentiated activities that meet individual requirements.

Assistive technology, tools, and programs

Many tools enable children with DS to access computers in various social settings. Therefore, if possible, the child must use the mouse and keyboard for learning, communication, and personal development. It was noted previously that children with profound and multiple disabilities or more complex and additional needs may not be able to use the mouse and keyboard. Still, there is a full range of assistive technology that should allow all children to access ICT.

Support learning for children with special educational needs hardware tools such as:

- Touch screen facilities may bridge the more commonly used input devices.
- Smart Screen as a flexible in lesson delivery and learning styles
- Mobile-ready learning and tablets
- Digital cameras, scanners, and printers can be used with computers to develop personalized resources and enhance activities.
- There are also various devices, such as joysticks, trackballs, and overlay keyboards.
- Augmentative AT tools include Special keyboards, alternative mice, switch buttons for alternative access to the computer, portable devices, and communication devices that create speech output.

Software: There is a large range of software and virtual reality programs to promote development in this area, including programs which focus on:

- Speech sounds and phonological awareness
- Sentence comprehension and storytelling
- Teaching reading to teach talking to support speech and language development
- A visual learning environment where audio feedback can be supported with text
- Bridge packages of speaking with support video clips
- Software packages to provide visual reminders of the items that the children with DS may be attempting to manipulate
- Programs for appealing graphics, animations, and music to increase interest and prolong attention
- Word processing to help a child with editing and presenting neat and accurate written work where the difficulties of handwriting produce frustration, hostility, and resentment

Listen, Look, Think, then Answer!

Teaching a child with Down Syndrome and learning difficulties

"Listen, Look, Think, then Answer" is my software program designed to teach children with Down syndrome and students with learning difficulties.

The program was developed in an Arabic environment, suitable for local environments, especially in the Arab communities, and tailor-made to meet the needs of children with DS to prompt learning skills and communication systems.

The program was designed in collaboration with specialists when we noted previously that traditional methods in educational tutorials were very primitive and had low attractiveness. Most teachers developed mainly lessons in Microsoft PowerPoint with low-quality statistic images and few interactions.

The program is divided into ten main sections: Listening, Identifying, Naming skills, Matching, Auditory Processing, Memory Enhancement, Reading and Vocabulary, Placement, and Direction. Memory enhancement drills, various basic vocabulary (common objects, colors, shapes, animals, arithmetic, etc.) exercises, computer use training, and speech-based activities.

The Listen, Look, Think, then Answer method offers various ways of overcoming differentiation-related problems. It allows teachers to produce individual worksheets, tasks to explore topics, and exercises to drill and practice without all the associated boredom. Studies suggest that the processing and recall of spoken information is improved when it is supported by relevant picture material. This information has led to educators stressing the importance of using visual supports, including pictures, signs, and print when teaching children with Down syndrome, as this approach fully uses their stronger visual memory skills. *"The program applied in Syria and the Sultanate of Oman.*

In disability-friendly environments at the age of 5G, softwarization is coming!

Standardization between advancing accessibility, 5G technologies, and Softwarization will remove all barriers for persons with disabilities.

Are we ready to remove all the barriers for persons with disabilities?

Shortly, robots, smart things, the Internet of Things (IoT), and machines will become the new "tools" directly controlled through 5G and Softwarization for helping persons with disabilities in daily lives, in their education, transport, and emergency services and employment, in the smart cities and at home, in social protection, participation equality and external action. Persons with disabilities will be in an inclusive environment with suitable, accessible, and quality services. This environment promises to deliver critically important applications and services to benefit humanity.

The smart environment is connected to the digitized individual and promises to deliver critically important applications and services to benefit humanity. Software-defined networking (SDN) and Network Function Virtualisation (NFV) should offer more agile networks that can provide everything from telemedicine to television, mobile banking to educational services in new and compelling ways globally.

The advent of 5G technologies and ICT networks signifies the next wave of a globally connected digital society. It creates a friendly and inclusive environment that empowers persons with disabilities to meet their needs and access public facilities.

"Softwarization" is a global systemic trend, appearing under the form of several technologies and models, such as Cloud Computing, Edge-Fog Computing (SDN), and (NFV), which share the same common denominator: "any transactions, functions, and services can be seen as applications executed on (virtual/logical resources hosted in) low cost distributed hardware." So, "Softwarization" is paving the way towards the 5G.

This wave of innovation will create a new future for people with disabilities, increasing their impact and overcoming the various environmental, social, and system barriers to seize opportunities and achieve their aspirations. New technologies will provide a smarter, more inclusive environment, allowing people with disabilities to participate and become more involved rather than being left out.

Cloud and Fog Computing (SDN) and (NFV) are just different facets of this same evolutionary trend, called the Softwarisation of infrastructures. There is no way to look at them separately. This trend will dramatically change the nature of telecommunications infrastructures by automating operations processes and increasing flexibility and programmability, reflecting directly on the lives of persons with disabilities and their families.

For example, mobile access to the internet, cloud-based services, and big data analytics are allowing persons with disabilities anywhere to leverage new kinds of globally connected and shared knowledge bases.

5 G-controlled robots are another excellent example of a potential future ecosystem. They will also allow the development and provision of cognition services for People with disabilities.

Smart cities combine a mix of machines and human traffic generated by various city-wide infrastructures; smart cities will become inclusive, "Disability-friendly environments" shortly.

5G technologies and Softwarization will make a massive difference to billions of people with disabilities worldwide. The global race is on to develop 5G, the fifth generation of mobile networks. While 5G will follow in the footsteps of 4G and 3G, scientists are more excited this time. They say 5G will be different—very different.

How emerging 5G technologies will interact in future networks to benefit persons with disabilities?

How do advancing accessibility and ICT accessibility experts plan for this new generation?

The new trend cannot be achieved unless an all-inclusive and accessible environment is created based on globally approved standards and infrastructure, systems, and technology improvements to achieve the initiative's vision of "disability friendly."

Where do innovation and accessibility meet?

Innovations enable persons with disabilities to achieve a more independent and worthwhile quality of life, empowering them to accept their right to social inclusion.

Innovation of accessibility is collaborating with all other agencies, industry organizations, and innovators to encourage and work with innovation and partnerships to enhance service users' lifestyles.

Accessibility and innovation are innovative design to inclusive design; accessible design generally benefits all users when integrated into the design process from the start.

Digital technologies and networks that connect people make it possible to create adaptable products and services that fit our human differences. Inclusive design can be seen as accessibility that benefits everyone and doesn't require one-size-fits-all, providing people access to IT and knowledge regardless of their abilities or disabilities.

Innovators and designers can't be experts in everyone's requirements. Digital tools and networks can democratize design, development, and production. This means we can become experts in our unique needs and participate in designing a system that will fit us. Inclusive design engages diverse perspectives, including those of the end user.

How can virtual worlds, geographic location apps, augmented reality, and the 3D Web possibly be adapted to users with disabilities, and how do we design for them?

How can we gain skills in policy design, interface design, software application specifications, rapid prototyping tools, 3D printers, and software development to make a virtual world a reality for persons with disabilities?

How can technology help improve our quality of life? Dr. Chieko Asakawa shows off some new technology that helps blind people explore the world more independently.

New technologies can promote greater independence for all.

IT companies are working on this issue for the broad range of individual human needs so everyone has equal access to digital knowledge through products and integrated accessibility. See case studies and IBM Accessibility research projects, examples of IBM-compliant product portfolios that, when used with IBM's associated documentation, satisfy the applicable requirements of Section 508 of the Rehabilitation Act.

Also, for the development community, Microsoft promoted accessibility innovation and worked with industry organizations to encourage innovation by reducing the complexity of accessible development and engaging in research and development. See more Microsoft Commitment to Accessibility.

The key elements are "Where do Innovation and Accessibility Meet? " and "What research is required to support accessibility as a component of innovation?"

Many persons with disabilities now have better and more independent access to information and communication. New technology developments can make this access easier and break barriers. These barriers can often be removed by considering the needs of disabled users when designing and implementing innovative and inclusive design.

Innovation is key to driving change across digital properties, for innovative accessibility to help identify, prototype and deliver creative ideas, from augmented reality through audio and touch technologies to partnering on driverless cars and digital guides.

We must include accessibility in innovation initiatives to promote collaborative problem-solving among stakeholders and ensure that persons with disabilities reap the full benefits of communications technology. The initiative fosters affordable technology solutions through workshops, field events, facilitated dialogues, and online tools.

Technologies are advancing rapidly; accessibility often plays a vital role with assistive tools in the latest innovations.

Innovation in Accessibility is usually built in the mode of action through developing products, standards, and regulations. Every industrial company is responsible for helping everyone contribute equally and doing the right thing. The positive impact of accessibility in technology products benefits all walks of life.

For example, CISCO tested products against U.S. standards, including Section 508 of the Rehabilitation Act, Section 255 of the Telecommunications Act, and the Americans with Disabilities Act. Cisco adheres to guidelines by the World Wide Web Consortium (W3C). It also contributed to accessibility standards and guidelines created by the International Telecommunications Union (ITU), the Internet Engineering Task Force (IETF), and the Telecommunications Industry Association (TIA). See Cisco, Accessibility: Our Responsibility

However, we are committed to accessibility regulations and standards. It's important to provide a solution that meets the needs of people with disabilities. We are also committed to working with accessibility experts and people with disabilities to design and build products that all people use—accessible products, hardware, software, and services that are now essential to business, education, government, and home communications.

Persons with disabilities in accessing and using the Internet, challenges and good practices

Accessing the Internet offers an opportunity for inclusiveness, to view the global community of its users as one while recognizing its rich diversity. Internet technologies can give persons with disabilities the means to live more equitably within the international community in a previously impossible manner.

The Internet empowers persons with disabilities to become more independent and participate in everyday activities such as employment, education, civic responsibilities, and social connections. Regardless of the challenges they may face, persons with disabilities can contribute to society like any other member of the community when barriers are removed. Increasing accessibility to the Internet can help to make that happen. Governments, industry, and other key stakeholders need to make accessibility a priority in their ongoing work, both individually and collaboratively. There is considerable discussion about the fact that the internet and other online services are new technologies that open up windows of opportunity for everyone to participate in the latest information age and that there are particular benefits and potentialities for persons with disabilities. This emphasis may reflect the broader goal of providing an "independent life."

However, there are also barriers and challenges facing persons with disabilities in accessing the Internet.

The different challenges facing persons with disabilities in accessing the internet, specifically in developing countries, can be identified in:

- Lack of awareness and interest in accessing the internet for persons with disabilities, specifically in rural areas in developing countries.
- Lack of necessary ICT accessibility tools and applications
- High cost for broadband connectivity, ICT accessibility, and assistive equipment.
- Lack of ongoing support and training on ICT accessibility. In addition, there are limited complementary Internet services, e.g., assistive technology, ICT accessibility tools software, and limited accessibility features at mainstream ICT training facilities.

- For Persons with disabilities, the potential benefit of access to the Internet is critically dependent on reliable, high-speed connectivity at affordable prices. For example, for people with hearing impairments who need high-quality video conferencing services for communication, the internet connection must be reliable and maintain high-quality real-time synchronized data speed.

- Affordable and reliable connectivity is a prerequisite for People with physical disabilities who need telework to maintain ongoing employment.

In this sense, the above-identified barriers can be seen as bottlenecks in using and accessing the Internet.

Challenges and good practices

- Encourage web developers; they should work to include accessibility in the design of the apps with technology, e.g., VoiceOver, record use of audio description, etc.

- Screen readers enable users with disabilities to hear the contents of a web page rather than read them; a screen reader can only read text, not images or animations. Therefore, images and animations must have text descriptions associated with them so the screen reader can read them. This text is called alternative text or "alt" text.

- A touch screen allows an individual to navigate the web page using hands without the fine motor control required by the mouse.

- The smartphone and tablet industry can develop the use of touchscreen devices with audio output specifically for visual media; in these cases, it is very important that essential components of the page work without a mouse.

- Develop mobile web design and accessibility to maximize the web's social, technical, financial, and legal benefits.

- Look to successful professional accessibility software developers and ask them how they learned and how they can build accessibility skills.

- Before beginning, an initiative decides how we can build and will affect the quality of the resulting accessibility.

- How can we address the lack of conformance to W3C guidelines and poor website design? Websites should be accessible and designed to comply with the W3C's AAA level, and AAA success criteria are defined in the Guidelines.

- Applying the legislative process to adopting a web accessibility policy, websites' online resources must balance and have accessible standards.

- Making websites accessible is useful for all persons with disabilities and those who are older, so we need to be compatible with alternate input devices, assistive technology, and software, and we should not forget the native languages.

- Build a group of qualified people and persons with disabilities within the online services company who can oversee accessibility projects. For example, recently, a new Chief Microsoft Accessibility Officer was appointed.

- We need to address the skills gap that prevents many persons with disabilities from using the internet.

- There is a need to implement innovative approaches to training and preparing persons with disabilities to use ICT accessibility and internet access.

- Efforts and cooperation to develop ICT skills programs to help persons with disabilities build their social media skills.

Few concrete programs truly provide the opportunity for equal access to persons with disabilities. Identifying and adopting accessibility standards to determine which standards apply to organizations and adopting those standards across the organizations, as the establishment of an approach to select tools and techniques to meet the needs and experience of the organizations.

Finally, there is a need for an initiative to expand access to the Internet to persons with disabilities, a principle, provisions to ensure not only affordability but also accessibility and usability for persons with disabilities through increased participation, education, and employment through deploying our efforts for achieving that specifically, in developing countries. We should look at the economic benefits of assimilating marginalized segments of society as a means of integration.

How can a baby with Down Syndrome learn, and what can they learn in the womb?

The ability of ICT to offer specific software in these areas is still outstanding.

Down's syndrome can be diagnosed before birth (prenatally). During pregnancy, two types of tests can be done to look for Down's syndrome: a screening test and a diagnostic test. To screen for Down syndrome, the dating scan and the nuchal translucency scan can be carried out simultaneously between 11 weeks and 13 weeks.

When the fetus reaches 23 weeks, recent research indicates that a variety of stimulation, while babies are in the womb is the start of building and promoting cognitive development. From playing music to reading to physical interaction in utero, stimulated babies can begin life with an advantage, being born with what some researchers consider more confidence in themselves and the ability to learn more easily. In addition to stimulating and purposefully interacting with the baby, staying relaxed and keeping stress levels at a minimum for the mother are also necessary for promoting fetal brain development.

The key question. Can these experiments also applied to fetuses with Down Syndrome?

Is a baby with Down syndrome ready to learn anything in the womb?

The test of learning can certainly help a baby's natural cognitive development by interacting with their mother, including singing and talking. According to several studies, reading stories, playing music, or even talking to a baby, the experience is a simple form of learning in the womb.

However, some experts say we can't rule out the possibility that learning happens after birth rather than before it. Also, even if teaching an unborn baby is possible, there's little proof that it has any long-lasting, beneficial effect.

How can a baby with Down Syndrome learn, and what can they learn in the womb?

Does this training program offer early intervention before birth (prenatally) and during pregnancy to help babies and toddlers with developmental delays or disabilities?

What training and technical assistance are provided, and is it helpful?

We know a child with Down syndrome has many problems with attention, concentration, learning, thinking, memory, perception, reading and writing.

So, what appropriate programs and software are available, and which would be particularly beneficial to pregnant mothers in the last three months of pregnancy?

There are three main ways that babies are thought to learn in the womb:

Learning by experience: Babies recognize familiar voices and music they heard in the womb and are soothed by them after birth.

For example, they are communicating, exploring, and thinking programs.

Learning by repetition: For example, training, communication, language, and reading stories via computer programs.

Learning by association: babies may learn to connect certain experiences to how they feel.

However, ICT's ability to offer specific software in these areas remains outstanding.

I also mention again what the experts say: A baby will probably be able to remember certain sounds and tastes from the womb after birth. When music is played to a baby in the womb, the baby's heart rate may increase and move more.

In the same way, the baby may also show recalls and is comforted by other noises heard while in the womb. These could be the theme tune of a favorite TV program or a story frequently read out loud. See (Will my baby learn anything in the womb?).

Sensory and brain mechanisms for hearing are developed at 30 weeks of gestational age, and the new study shows that unborn babies are listening to their mothers talk during the last 10 weeks of pregnancy and at birth can demonstrate what they've heard. There's no evidence that experiences can increase a baby with Down Syndrome development skills. However, hearing a voice may help the baby recognize and bond with the mother after birth.

"The mother has first dibs on influencing the child's brain," said Patricia Kuhl, co-author and co-director of the Institute for Learning & Brain Sciences at the University of Washington. "The vowel sounds in her speech are the loudest units, and the fetus locks onto them."

Through the deep search, I couldn't find and reach any information on this study about cognitive development for fetuses with Down syndrome, but it was just a suggestion to many developmental experts, researchers, and pediatricians; maybe they could find possible solutions for this idea!

References and Related Posts

Teleworking: Is this option right for the employment of persons with disabilities

Work At Home/Telework as a Reasonable Accommodation

Best Practices for Employers

Accessible ICT in Successful Telecommuting Strategies

Teleworktools.org

Where Can I Find Information about Working from Home/Telework?

Accessible banking to persons with disabilities

- *Look at Internet Banking Accessibility in Australia, AUSTRALIAN BANKERS' ASSOCIATION,* http://ausweb.scu.edu.au/aw04/papers/refereed/celic/paper.html
- *Inclusive financial services for seniors and persons with disabilities: Global Trends in Accessibility Requirements". G3ict*
- *Apple Bank for Savings*
- *Disabled People's Association, Access to Banking Services Seminar, VOX NOSTRA, 2013*
- *Center for Financial Inclusion at ACCION International (2013), Key to the Future, Financial Inclusion and Opportunity for all. Concept note for panel discussion. Retrieved November 20, 2014, from:*

  http://www.un.org/disabilities/documents/idpd/idpd2013_financialinclusionpanel.pdf

Accessibility and the future of the Internet of Things

W3C, Internet of Things

 "Google: IoT Can Help The Disabled."

Internet of Things: New Promises for Persons with Disabilities

The Internet of Things Could Empower People with Disabilities

Internet of Things (IoT) and People with Disabilities

Telecare, assistive technology, and ICT accessibility for persons with dementia

- *Alzheimers.net,* http://www.alzheimers.net
- *Health Victoria, http://www.health.vic.gov.au/*
- *iCareHealth, Technology supporting Care, How assistive technology can help to improve dementia care, http://www.icarehealth.co.uk/blog/assistive-technology-improve-dementia-care*
- *Social Care for Excellence's Assistive Technology for Older People,* http://www.scie.org.uk/publications/briefings/files/briefing28.pdf

Accessible e-learning platforms, hopes, and challenges!

Accessibility for E-Learning: Section 508 and WCAG

Section 508 Standards for Electronic and Information Technology

Accessibility to E-Learning for Persons With Disabilities: Strategies, Guidelines, and Standards

Disability and eLearning: Opportunities and Barriers

ICT accessibility and employment of persons with disabilities

United Nations Department of Public Information

UN Enable: Factsheet on Persons with Disabilities

ILO Global Business and Disability Network

Employment and Social Development Canada

The ICT Opportunity for a Disability-Inclusive Development Framework

Lunch and Learn: Assistive Technology in the Workplace

Tourism destinations and accessibility for persons with disabilities

The Manual on Accessible Tourism for All: Public-Private Partnerships and Good Practices

Rights of Tourists with Disabilities in the European Union Framework

Barrier-Free Tourism for People with Disabilities in the Asian and Pacific Region

Library services and accessibility of eBooks for persons with disabilities

- *International Federation of Library Associations and Institutions IFLA Professional Reports, No. 89 Access to libraries for persons with disabilities.*
- *Accessible Publishing, Best Practice Guidelines for Publishers, 2013, EDItEUR*
- *Building Free Library for Universal Accessibility, Australian Library and Information Association, ALIA*

Useful web address: DAISY Consortium, Accessible EPUB 3, IDPF Guidelines

Accessibility to strengthen arts and culture for persons with disabilities

Expanding the Arts: Deaf and Disability Arts, Access and Equality Strategy

Shape Arts: Opportunities and support for disabled artists and cultural organizations to build a more inclusive and representative cultural sector

The National Endowment for the Arts Office for Accessibility:

Section 504 Self-Evaluation Workbook

The North Carolina Arts Council

ICT accessibility in the education of children with Down syndrome

About Down syndrome

The UK Down's Syndrome Association, Down Syndrome Education Online

Down Syndrome Ireland

Down syndrome: good practice guidelines for education, All Party Parliamentary Group on Down Syndrome, Education Advisory Group 2012

Learners with Down syndrome, Down Syndrome Victoria, March 2009, A Handbook for Teaching Professionals

Where innovation and accessibility meet